D0806087

Port Washington Public Library
One Library Drive
Port Washington, NY 11050
(516) 883-4400   FEB 06 2018

STONEHENGE

STONEHENGE

THE STORY OF A SACRED LANDSCAPE

Francis Pryor

PEGASUS BOOKS
NEW YORK LONDON

omtrent IIII.LXXX van syne edelen: Maer de ...
hebbende hen seluer voorsien med Wapenen ende ghewee... wilt
zy onder hun mantelen droeghen, verstoeghen alle dese
Britanen ende naemen den Coningh ghevanghen Aurelius
Ambrosius die naer Votigern Coningh werdt. Willende de
verslegher Britaensche edele een eeuwyghe ghedynckenisse
oprechten dede door de behendicheyt van Merlyn eenen
grooten hoop steenen rommen uut Irland ende dede die
stellen op S. Ambrosius berch, die so noch staen In deser
voeghe, soo Ick seluer ter plaetsen uut ghewerckent
hebbe.

FOR GEOFF WAINWRIGHT,
WHOSE INNOVATIVE RESEARCH
INTO HENGES HAS INSPIRED
TWO GENERATIONS

PROLOGUE
WHY STONEHENGE MATTERS
— 10 —

INTRODUCTION
RELIGION, LANDSCAPE
AND CHANGE
— 16 —

1
AFTER THE ICE
[8000–4000 BC]
— 28 —

2
THE STONEHENGE
'RITUAL LANDSCAPE'
[4000–1500 BC]
— 46 —

3
BEFORE THE GREAT STONES,
PART I:
THE FORMATIVE STAGE
[FROM 3300 BC]
— 68 —

4
BEFORE THE GREAT STONES,
PART II:
STAGE I [FROM 3000 BC]
— 80 —

5

THE GREAT STONES ARRIVE:
STAGE 2 [FROM 2500 BC]
— 98 —

6

THE JOURNEY FROM LIFE
TO DEATH:
STAGE 3 [FROM 2400 BC]
— 124 —

7

LATER DEVELOPMENTS:
STAGES 4 AND 5 [2100–1500 BC]
— 140 —

8

AFTER THE STONES
— 154 —

9

STONEHENGE TODAY
— 170 —

APPENDIX I
TIMELINE OF SIGNIFICANT
EVENTS IN
BRITISH PREHISTORY
— 182 —

APPENDIX II
THE DITCH AND
THE GRADUAL ESTABLISHMENT
OF STONEHENGE
— 186 —

NOTES
— 202 —

ACKNOWLEDGEMENTS
— 199 —

INDEX
— 206 —

PICTURE CREDITS
— 208 —

PROLOGUE:
WHY STONEHENGE MATTERS

Stonehenge is an extraordinary monument in its own right. Its massive shaped stones and unique lintels instantly catch one's attention and hold it. It was constructed at a time when British and north European prehistoric* societies were passing through a crucially important phase of development. Sites like Stonehenge provided the stability that enabled communities of the third millennium BC to take Britain from a developing to an established social system with more clearly defined regional identities. It was a period which saw the population grow, supported by improved and more intensive farming. This in turn led to a developed landscape, which was serviced by a complex infrastructure of roads, paths, streams, rivers, farms and settlements.

In this book I will try to show how Stonehenge formed an integral part of the quite rapidly evolving social and ideological system of the time. And we should bear in mind that although the site would always have been very special, it was never a one-off – although unique in its complexity and construction, it was always part of a broader and widespread tradition of British stone and timber monuments. Just like a medieval cathedral today, it would have been awe-inspiring but comprehensible to a person in the Neolithic or Bronze Age. Much later, when that understanding of its purpose and role had vanished, it acquired a mystical/magical quality that even recent research has found hard to shift.

There have been many books written about Stonehenge and most of them say something new. Recently the Stonehenge landscape has been the subject of intensive research by a number of projects, all of which have made significant discoveries.[1] In this book I will draw heavily, for example, on the Stonehenge Riverside Project, organized by Mike Parker Pearson of University College London and by colleagues in the universities of Bournemouth, Manchester and Southampton. The science of geophysics uses radar and other impulses to 'see' below the surface and several teams of

---

* I use the terms 'prehistory' and 'prehistoric' to describe the people, places and events that took place in Britain before the arrival of the Romans in AD 43.

prospectors, organized by English Heritage and the Stonehenge Hidden Landscapes Project, among others, have made some truly astonishing discoveries.

I will of course cover this new research as best I can, but what, it might reasonably be asked, do I bring to this richly covered table? Here I have to confess that my own research and experience in British prehistory has been largely confined to the low-lying Fenlands of eastern England – landscapes that could hardly be less like those of Salisbury Plain or the Marlborough Downs. True, I have excavated henges, but these were made of wood, not stone, and cannot readily be compared with Stonehenge. Having said that, they also occurred within larger, so-called 'ritual landscapes' (see Chapter 3), that do have much closer parallels with what was happening on Salisbury Plain.

I suppose my most relevant experience came from the excavation of a site known as a causewayed enclosure. Etton was excavated in great detail between 1982 and 1987 and it still remains the best-preserved site of its kind yet found in Britain (it is discussed extensively in Chapter 3 and Appendix II). Causewayed enclosures are several centuries earlier than places like Stonehenge, but they were the first communal shrines and meeting places in prehistoric Europe and they hold the clues to the powerful motives that made early communities come together and construct a huge variety of barrows, henges and other ceremonial sites. These individual sites formed the basic building blocks of the ritual landscapes that would later develop from and around them. And as we will see throughout this book, Stonehenge lay at the centre of the largest and probably the most complex ritual landscape in Britain.[2]

All archaeologists approach their subject from their own perspective, and while I have tried not to let my interest in the origins of Stonehenge bias this book unnecessarily, I also feel I owe it to my readers to give them fresh insights into this most remarkable site. I have to say that I think current theories on the origins of Stonehenge, during a single 'event', which happened around 2900 BC, are misguided and ignore what we have learnt about the previous millennium of prehistory. So I have suggested here that there was an extended 'Formative Phase' that was at least four centuries long (Chapter 4 and Appendix II). I rather suspect that although this length of time accords with currently available radiocarbon dates, future research may demonstrate that it was an underestimate.

Francis Pryor

INTRODUCTION:
RELIGION, LANDSCAPE
AND CHANGE

Stonehenge was erected during times of extraordinary change that still profoundly affect the way we live our lives in Europe to this day. And its construction was no accident. Sacred sites like Stonehenge played an important part in providing the social stability that allowed later prehistoric communities to accept and adopt such major innovations as the appearance of the first metals, copper and bronze.

The mysterious but iconic ring of stones on Salisbury Plain that today we call Stonehenge has long been recognized as an ancient shrine or religious site. But it would be a mistake to suggest that prehistoric Britons viewed religion in the same way that we do today.[3] A lot has happened since those far-off times. For a start, the diversity of religions that we now enjoy would not have applied in prehistory. It would also be a mistake to believe that prehistoric Britain – indeed prehistoric Europe – never changed, or changed very slowly. In fact, the opposite is the case: all modern research is suggesting that the nine millennia that comprise Britain's later prehistory were times of near-continuous population growth, which witness the development of houses, farms, villages, tracks, roads, woodland and fields. By 2000 BC sophisticated sea-going vessels were making regular, perhaps daily, trips across the Channel and southern North Sea. And by the final centuries BC we see the appearance of larger communities that are starting to resemble towns.

Human settlement on the north-European landmass that was later to become the British Isles extends back over a million years to the Old Stone Age, or Palaeolithic. In this book, however, we will confine our attention to the ten thousand or so years that followed the end of the final Ice Age around 10,000 BC. For convenience, archaeologists have subdivided this enormous length of time into four main periods and one shorter transitional period (see Appendix I):

The Mesolithic (10,000–4200 BC)
The Neolithic (4000–2500 BC)
The British Copper Age, or Chalcolithic (2500–2200 BC)
The Bronze Age (2200–800 BC)
The Iron Age (800 BC–AD 43)

Each of these periods witnessed a major change that has left clear traces in the archaeological record. For example, the Mesolithic (or Middle Stone Age) was the final period in British prehistory when people survived by hunting and by foraging, or gathering, their food from natural sources. So they developed specialized spears, arrows and digging sticks that made the processes of hunting and foraging more efficient. Their spears and arrows were tipped with small, sharp blades that they fashioned from flints. These flint blades are known as microliths and are very characteristic of the Mesolithic period. By way of contrast, in the following Neolithic (or New Stone Age) period, which is marked by the arrival of the first farmers along the southern shores of Britain in the two or so centuries prior to 4000 BC, the arrowheads are much larger and shaped in subtly different ways. This difference in the shape and style of flint implements allows archaeologists to distinguish between the first two periods in their excavations.

The final three ages of later prehistory are defined by major technological changes: first, the introduction of copper, followed just three centuries later by the development of bronze (an alloy of copper with tin) and then the appearance of the first iron tools, shortly after 800 BC. The Copper Age, or Chalcolithic, can also be recognized on the continental mainland – it is labelled as 'British' here because of its unique social and religious developments, which are very much in evidence at Stonehenge.

These major changes of lifestyle were not accompanied by huge influxes of new people. By 4000 BC British hunters and foragers were becoming very adept at managing their game and at conserving their natural food resources, such as hazelnuts. And we know that from around 9000 BC they had domesticated dogs from wolves. So the post-Ice Age hunters were not as profoundly different from the first farmers who succeeded them, in around 4000 BC, as was once believed – and that probably explains why the idea of farming spread so fast, right across Britain, reaching northern Scotland by 3800 BC.[4]

The final three ages of later prehistory are named after changes in metal-working. These, too, may have been introduced by new arrivals, but the proportion of these newcomers to Britain would have been far smaller than the numbers of pioneer farmers. So the archaeological periods do not necessarily signal major changes or disruptions in the way human societies and communities lived their lives or organized the landscape. And as we will see at Stonehenge, shared religious and spiritual beliefs helped communities remain united while they adapted to the new technological and social developments.

In the recent past many archaeologists believed that the move from hunting and foraging to farming around 4000 BC was nothing short of a cultural revolution. Thanks to sites like Stonehenge we now realize that these lifestyle changes were certainly important, but they were adopted by societies that had been in existence for some five millennia. One might have expected, for example, to have seen monuments like Stonehenge erected in new places. Indeed that often happened, but sometimes particularly important monuments were erected on sites that had been spiritually significant for a very long time previously. As we will see, recent research has clearly demonstrated that the landscape around Stonehenge would have been widely accepted as emotionally and religiously important, both by Mesolithic hunters of early post-Ice Age times, and by farmers of the Neolithic and Early Bronze Ages, some six millennia later. Put another way, places like Stonehenge would have been perceived as abiding symbols of spiritual and cultural continuity.

Religions in prehistoric times differed quite profoundly from their modern Western equivalents. Today we tend to organize our lives into a series of structured 'boxes'. Very busy people even talk about special 'quality time' – often a few hours at weekends – when they can enjoy the company of their partners and children. This provides a contrast with the rest of their week when the worlds of work and recreation are kept firmly apart. Religion, too, is treated in this way: if one is a believer, one goes to church on Sunday,

An engraving of a map of
Wiltshire by Jodocus
Hondius from John Speed's
*Theatre of the Empire of Great
Britain*, published in 1611.

and one takes one's family. Indeed, the church in the Western world today
sees itself as a symbol of family stability. This is also its strongest link to the
religious practices of previous times.

Almost nobody in the modern West would build or maintain an altar,
let alone a chapel, at home. At most, a religious devotee might say prayers
before going to bed. And of course the reason for this is that religion in the
modern Western world has ceased to be a part of daily life. For some, it
may still have a role, but this is clearly limited to certain times and places.
So it is very difficult for many of us to imagine a time when the mental
compartments of modern life – work, gym, commute, relaxation,
recreation, mealtime, bedtime for the children, etc., etc. – were non-
existent. All activities were viewed as part of something much larger. In
prehistory the practicalities of daily life may have been simpler at a purely
functional level, but people have always had active minds. So they created
rich spiritual and ideological worlds. These imagined realms were more
than mere myth and fantasy, because they were based on observable facts
and phenomena. Stories of the ancestors, for example, may well have been
constructed around the lives of real people. Tales such as these would have
helped hold larger family-based groups, like clans, tribes and chiefdoms,
together.

Other ideas and observations helped to shape the now rapidly evolving
concepts of social awareness and spiritual identity. For example, natural
occurrences, such as eclipses, or the rising and setting of the sun and moon at
key times of the year, were carefully observed and could be predicted with
remarkable precision. Many prehistoric sites, including Stonehenge, are
arranged around the midwinter or midsummer solstices.* It has been
suggested that this meant they were used as a means of computing or
calculating such celestial events. More recent opinion favours a less specific,

---

* The midsummer and midwinter solstices mark the longest and shortest days of the year: 21
June and 21 December. The spring and autumn equinoxes (21 March and 21 September) are the
mid-points between the two solstices.

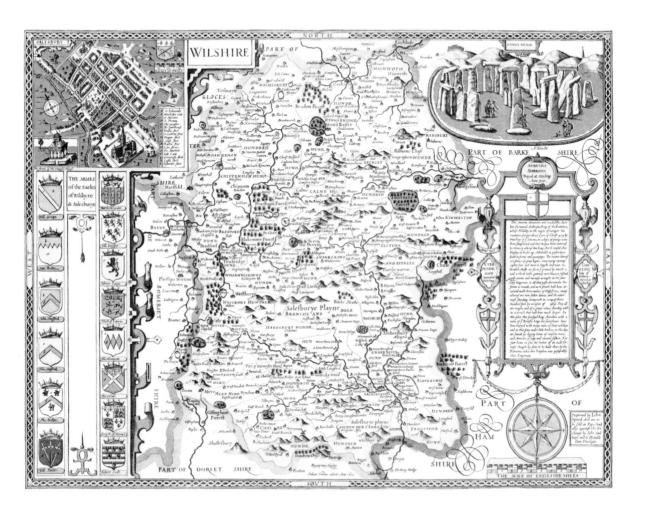

more general explanation. Today prehistoric shrines with these celestial alignments are seen as links to the wider natural world. The passage of the sun determines day length and season, both of which were of fundamental importance to foragers and farmers alike.

Prehistoric people also had a different concept of time. Today we view what happened during the passing of hours, days and weeks as a non-repeatable chain of unique events. Essentially our concept of time is linear: with a beginning, a middle and an end. So books such as this feature time*lines*, which show how the world has gradually changed over past years, centuries or millennia (Appendix I). We see our lives in terms of hours, days, months and years, each one of which has a number. But in the ancient and not-so-distant past, rural people viewed time in terms of cycles. Numbers were less important. Years may well have been named, as they are still in many parts of the world. What mattered, and gave structure to people's lives, was the annual passage of the seasons. This of course was a repetitive, cyclical, process and was fundamentally different from linear perceptions of time. In fact, many domestic houses in later prehistory were laid out in a way that reflected the daily passage of the sun – yet another cyclical process. Sometimes altars were placed opposite the front door, which was positioned to let in the light of dawn and early morning. This cyclical view of time gave form and structure to the way people perceived religion and the greater cycle of their own lives. It also explains why so many prehistoric monuments – including Stonehenge, of course – were based on rings or circles.

Religion and ideas about the spiritual world united all aspects of people's lives: they gave structure to their surroundings and may well have explained where they were to spend their time after death. As we have seen, the passing of the seasons gave form to the farming year. Similarly, in death, the ancestors played a role in parcelling up the landscape of the living: different holdings, maybe of families or villages, were marked out by burial mounds, or sometimes by individual graves. So the dead could be seen as playing a practical role in the day-to-day lives of people working on the land. Religion was also the basis of family life and its myths gave credence to sagas of the ancestors. In short, shared beliefs underpinned everything, from tribal politics to the most trivial aspects of domestic life. The stability these spiritual ideas provided was of fundamental importance to everyone in society, which might help explain why shrines like Stonehenge were constructed with such extraordinary skill, and Herculean labour.

But pre-Roman religion differed from its modern counterpart in another, more subtle way, which has only recently been recognized by prehistorians. When modern research into Stonehenge began at the start of the twentieth century, it very soon became apparent that it was not going to be a simple story to unravel. If the stones and the subtle remains of ditches and banks look complex on the surface, it is as nothing to what lies below the ground. As time passed, and as more and more religious sites broadly similar to Stonehenge (like, for example, the nearby complex at Avebury) began to be examined in greater detail it became increasingly apparent that they all shared this extraordinary complexity.[5] It was as if the constructors of these great monuments were never satisfied with their work and spent their entire lives tweaking and fiddling with their creations. Now we know from the 14,000 or so medieval parish churches that are such an enduring feature of the British landscape, that during the Middle Ages architects and builders would be called in to modify or enlarge these buildings, but it was never done with the frequency and thoroughness that we can observe at places like Stonehenge and Avebury.

As time passed, further complexities were revealed at numerous Neolithic and early Bronze Age religious sites and landscapes right across Britain, from the Orkney Islands, to Ireland and southern England. By the 1970s and 1980s, prehistorians began to understand that there was more to the complexity they were revealing on their excavations than merely a sense of perfectionism in the remote past. It was then realized that these ancient shrines were not like churches – their modern equivalents – at all. Their pattern of use was entirely different.

In historical and modern times, Christian churches were first built, and were then sanctified with an elaborate religious ceremony. At that point they became the House of God where all may come and worship. In other words, the building was first completed and was then sanctified and opened for business. The process of building may well have taken a long time, and there would be later modifications, but it was most unusual for a church to close once it had been acknowledged as the House of God. And it did not take long before prehistorians realized that the way prehistoric shrines like Stonehenge were used was very different. It was soon appreciated that the stones and ditches of the 'building' at Stonehenge were not, of themselves, the focus of ancient worship. Instead, people came there to experience and to be a part of a very special place in the landscape. The stage-by-stage erection of the many stones that today comprise the world-famous monument was their way of expressing their respect for the sacred or mystical landscape where it stands – and for what that symbolized. Indeed, in many instances, the builders and the worshippers might well have been the same people. The great stones were never meant to form a building that was constructed, finished, sanctified and then opened for use. Put another way, the seemingly ceaseless building and rebuilding that we can now work out in some detail was, in fact, the shrine's actual 'use'. When people came to Stonehenge they wanted to make their mark, either as individuals or as communities. And often they did this by altering it in some way. Sometimes, as we will see in subsequent chapters, the works were so demanding that dozens of different communities must have come together to perform the hard labours they required. Other times the changes were small, or even tiny – such as the carving of a bronze axehead on a stone (Chapter 8).

So was Stonehenge ever 'finished'? The answer to that has to be no, because completion was never the intention of the people who created it. I do believe, however, that the main elements, the great Sarsen Circle and the Trilithon Horseshoe were completed, as these probably symbolized the sacred landscape itself. They would have provided the formal, stable setting for the other, more transitory changes that took place around them.

In later prehistory it often seems that the process of doing things, mattered more than the final product. And this, of course, makes perfect sense if your pattern of thought is based on cycles rather than finished end-products. Today we would see ourselves as more rational, if less imaginative. To us, objectives, goals and 'targets' are everything. But we should also have the humility to learn from the past. There are other ways of experiencing life. When we see the extraordinary complex of monuments that comprise the Stonehenge landscape we are witnessing the way ancient people perceived their world and its realities. It is an amazing privilege. So we must never underestimate the many dimensions, layers and infinite subtleties of what their imaginations have bequeathed to us. The great stones and the landscape around them are telling us a complex and a very human story, too, doubtless complete with its fair share of dead ends and inconsistencies. Consequently, simple one-off explanations, such as 'Stonehenge was a computer', 'Stonehenge was about sun worship' or 'Stonehenge was created by a powerful leader' are not just misleading; they insult the intelligence of the thousands of men and women who created this extraordinary and timeless monument.

If we are ever to appreciate the powerful motives that inspired people to create Stonehenge, we must first turn the clock back some ten thousand years. That is the only way we will discover why this corner of Salisbury Plain became so special in the hearts and minds of prehistoric people. But we are now entering a very remote and sometimes rather hostile world. The last Ice Age has just ended, and the British Isles have yet to separate from mainland Europe. Momentous events are about to take place.

[overleaf]
An aerial photograph of Stonehenge.

I

AFTER THE ICE
[8000–4000 BC]

Humans abandoned the areas of northwestern Europe that were later to become the British Isles during the coldest spells of the Ice Ages. By about 10,000 BC conditions had become somewhat warmer; glaciers, for example, had all retreated, but not enough to tempt people to return. But all that was to change around 9600 BC, when the climate suddenly warmed by some ten degrees Celsius. This remarkable event took place over a very short time – maybe the lifetimes of just two or three generations.[6] In fact, there is scientific evidence to suggest that by 8000 BC the climate may have been slightly warmer than it is today.[7]

The warming climate led to the melting of polar and glacial ice, as it is still doing today. Melting ice caused sea levels to rise and by 8000 BC the North Sea was becoming a substantial feature – the British and Irish coastlines were already much as they are now, with the exception of the south and east of England, from Yorkshire to the Isle of Wight. These flatter landscapes were linked to a coastal plain that extended out into the North Sea between the Humber and the Thames estuary. At the centre of what is now the southern North Sea was a low-lying, marshy plain of gently undulating low hills, known as 'Doggerland' (after the Dogger Bank).[8] By the time the first farmers arrived in Britain, shortly before 4000 BC, Britain had been separated from the continental mainland for some two millennia and Doggerland now lay below a shallow sea.

The traditional view of life in Britain after the Ice Ages is essentially bleak: a slight improvement on the Flintstones-style 'cavemen' way of life (itself something of a myth), but not much better. In reality, the post-Ice Age world was a great deal richer and more abundant than had previously been imagined. We now know that the number of people who returned to what by 9000 BC were the rapidly forming British Isles was substantial, and certainly much larger than had been thought in the 1950s and 1960s. But then something most remarkable happened. In December 1969 oil was discovered beneath the seabed off the Norwegian coast at Ekofisk; later in the same month another oilfield was revealed in the North Sea, some 135 miles (217 km) east of Aberdeen. These discoveries caused a new oil boom. This boom involved intensive geological prospection, which was carried out by the different oil companies, using three-dimensional seismic survey. Initially this information was very commercially confidential, but early in the twenty-first century it was made available to archaeologists who, unlike the geologists, were interested in the layers immediately below the seabed.

When the archaeologists examined the survey data they were able to show that Doggerland was far from an inhospitable, muddy marsh.[9] In fact, it must have provided Mesolithic people with a wealth of natural resources, including huge quantities of fish, shellfish and wildfowl. There were vast beds of reeds for thatching roofs, while wood for fuel and timber would have been available on higher ground, where game could also be hunted. The lush plains and rich fisheries of Doggerland must have seemed much more attractive than the austere uplands of Britain, just visible on the far horizon. But as time passed, sea levels continued their relentless rise and people were forced to seek drier land in ever-increasing numbers.

Initially people sought out landscapes that were broadly similar to the plains of the southern North Sea basin. In fact, the earliest of these settlements to be discovered was at Star Carr on low-lying, sometimes marshy land around the fringes of the now-drained glacial lake Flixton, in northeast Yorkshire, south of Scarborough, some 4 miles (6 km) from the coast. The site was first excavated just after the Second World War, when it was thought to be a superbly well-preserved temporary hunting camp. We now know that it was far, far more than that. Indeed, it has subsequently revealed more about life in post-Ice Age Britain, than any other site. The dig originally made national news when several antler headdresses, fashioned from the tops of red deer skulls, were discovered. Recent excavations have exposed a permanent settlement, including the remains of the earliest house to have been found in Britain. This house, which dates to around 9000 BC, was a substantial oval structure measuring just over

4 metres (13 ft) across, with a shallow, 20-centimetre (8-in) deep sunken floor, also roughly oval, but slightly smaller (3 metres or 10 feet) at the centre. The floor had been made-up with reeds, bark and brushwood and there was evidence for a central hearth. The walls were supported on posts, which had been sunk into the ground; their circular post-holes survived clearly as dark stains in the sandy sub-soil. But the evidence which proved beyond doubt that this was indeed the site of a house was the dense concentration of flint tools and fragments of bone, which followed the outline of the roof – this was probably made from reed thatch (the more familiar straw thatch of modern Britain had to await the arrival of farming some 5,000 years later).

The Star Carr settlement was far larger than anyone had imagined for so early a site. It covered some 20,000 square metres (about 5 acres or 2 hectares).[10] Currently the best estimates suggest there were between ten and thirty houses there at any one time. In essence, then, this was a small village of 200–400 inhabitants and the preserved environmental evidence indicates it was permanently occupied, all the year round, in two separate episodes. The first of these lasted about 80 years, then there was a gap of a century, followed by a second, and final, occupation of 150 years. Ongoing research shows clearly that there were other settlements around Lake Flixton. Of course, we can only make an informed guess at this stage, but a population of over 1,000 people around the lake seems likely. It is quite possible that ten to fifteen times this population lived in the surrounding and lower-lying parts of northeast Yorkshire. And there is no reason to suppose that similar populations should not be found in comparable places elsewhere in Britain. Indeed, the valley and floodplain of the River Avon, near Stonehenge, is just such an area.

Archaeologists have long realized that we will never understand why Stonehenge was built unless we view it in its wider landscape setting. This is because the famous site does not sit in splendid isolation. It is surrounded by literally hundreds of prehistoric monuments, many of which can be clearly seen from the air and indeed from the ground too. Modern visitors can see a selection of them if they take the bus from the Visitor Centre to the site. Better still, if they take a walk of a few hundred yards in any direction from the Visitor Centre, they can inspect one or two at their leisure. But many are not visible to the naked eye, as they still lie beneath the ground, buried by centuries of soil growth. The best way to reveal these 'invisible' monuments is by modern techniques of geophysical prospection, such as ground-penetrating radar and aerial survey. Two of the best clues that the Stonehenge landscape was regarded as special from very early times indeed were found by excavation. The first was in advance of modern construction work, the second during a research project. But neither was expected, and each came as a complete surprise.

In 1966 it was decided to enlarge the car park to cope with increasing numbers of visitors. Today this is the area where the shuttle buses turn round and collect passengers for the return journey, but in those days the route that the shuttle bus now takes from the Visitor Centre to Stonehenge was a public highway, the old Amesbury to Shrewton road, or A344. This road was closed as part of the building of the new Visitor Centre, which opened to the public in December 2013. Being so close to the monument, the area of the car park extension was excavated by two very experienced archaeologists and to the highest standards.[11] They revealed four pit-like features, almost equally spaced out and arranged in a row some 35 metres (115 ft) long, which was aligned precisely east–west. When first exposed they must have looked like the foundations for a row of smaller stone posts, similar to the Bluestones (see Chapter 5) of the neighbouring monument. But after excavation they proved to be very different. The most westerly pit was a root-hole where a tree had grown, or been grown. The three pits to the east had all been dug to hold substantial posts of about 75 centimetres (2½ ft) diameter – that's roughly the size of a large modern telegraph pole. Normally one would expect such posts to have been made from oak, which is hard and naturally resists rot, but when examined in the laboratory, the charcoal proved to be pine. Somewhat later, radiocarbon dates were taken from the pine charcoal found at the base of the pits.

Everyone expected the car park dates to be contemporary with the huge Stones* just across the A344, but they were not. In fact, they were almost twice as old, falling between about 7000 and 8000 BC. At the time, it was said that this range of years proved that the three huge posts could never have been standing together at the same time. We now realize, however, that some of the charcoal could have come from the centre, the oldest part, of a growing tree and some could have come from below the bark; this was wood which had just formed when the tree was felled – and there could be hundreds of years between the two. It is also worth noting that the early radiocarbon dates explain the choice of pine, because in the eighth millennium BC oak trees had yet to recolonize southern Britain after the retreat of the Ice Age glaciers.

Today it is accepted that the car park trench had indeed exposed a row of earlier Mesolithic posts, even if some of them might have been replaced or renewed. But their regular spacing and careful arrangement in a row, together with the radiocarbon dates, strongly suggested that this was a deliberate, and very early construction. This sense of careful planning was confirmed, if not simplified, by the discovery of yet another pit in a further extension to the car park, in 1988. The new find was about 100 metres (109 yd) east of the tree and the three post-holes, but it was some 20 metres (22 yd) south of the previous east–west alignment. The pit had probably held a big post, too, but had been redug slightly later. A large fragment of pine charcoal from the bottom of the redug layers gave a radiocarbon date of 8090–7690 BC.† It was contemporary with the others – and doubtless further early pits remain to be discovered.

---

* To avoid unnecessary repetition, 'Stones' will sometimes be substituted for 'Stonehenge'.

† Radiocarbon dates are never absolutely precise and are quoted as a range of years. The smaller or less reliable the sample, the greater the quoted range. The range quoted here is quite close, given the sample's considerable age.

So what was going on at Stonehenge around 8000 BC? Even the best-informed archaeologists were puzzled by the row of pits: perhaps the pine posts had been erected as part of a huge defensive work? But this idea was immediately rejected: the landscape is flat and would have been indefensible without a major earthwork of some sort, such as a deep ditch or steep bank. Widely spaced posts on their own would not have been sufficient.

Could they have formed part of a building? Even though the very early house at Star Carr had yet to be discovered, a number of Mesolithic dwellings had been found, so archaeologists were well aware of their general shape and size, which was very much smaller than the pine posts.[12] Accordingly, archaeological opinion was firmly agreed that the car park posts could not have served any practical purpose. Viewed from a modern perspective, this apparent lack of practical purpose allowed only one possible explanation: 'ritual' – the term prehistorians use to describe the 'impractical' realms of religion, ideology and belief.

For over forty years the huge pine posts remained an awkward and unsatisfactorily explained part of the Stonehenge story. Then, in 2008, something remarkable happened. But to find out who did what, we must first introduce the Stonehenge Riverside Project.

The early twenty-first century AD has witnessed an extraordinary blossoming of research into Stonehenge and its landscape. Many new approaches have been adopted, including advanced geophysical prospection for ancient features below the ground, detailed digital scanning of the stones and limited excavation. Given the fact that Stonehenge was extensively excavated in the twentieth century, all further disturbance of the ground must be severely restricted to ensure below-ground deposits remain untouched for future research.[13] But the Stonehenge Riverside Project adopted a variety of different approaches to tackle a series of clearly defined questions.[14] Although disciplined, their approach was also flexible. This open-minded attitude enabled Professor Mike Parker Pearson and his team to make some remarkable discoveries that have transformed our

AFTER THE ICE

understanding of the purpose and age of this unique site. The project began in 2003 and lasted for seven years, until the last season of excavations in 2009.

In later prehistoric times, Stonehenge was approached by a processional way marked out by a parallel bank and ditch on either side. This route is known as the Avenue. Today the banks and ditches of the Avenue are not very deep, but they are clearly visible on the surface, and particularly from the air. As it approaches the Stones, the Avenue is on a northeast–southwest alignment. Modern visitors, however, reach Stonehenge from the northwest and therefore do not encounter its original entrance until they have completed the circular walk around the Stones. About 500 metres (545 yd) away from the Stones, at a place known as the elbow, the straight alignment curves southwards towards the River Avon. This slightly circuitous route suggests two things. First, that a north-easterly approach was important and, second, that the river, too, played a significant role in the ancient ceremonies. We will discuss these matters in Chapters 5 and 6, but here all we need to note is that both the final 500 metres of the Avenue and the stones of Stonehenge itself are arranged on that same northeast–southwest alignment. That alignment is precisely the same as the direction of midsummer sunrise and midwinter sunset: the longest and shortest days of the year, otherwise known as the midsummer and midwinter solstices.

One way of limiting the impact of archaeological investigation on precious ancient deposits is to reopen trenches that have been excavated in earlier times. In 2008 the Riverside Project team re-excavated a trench across the Avenue that had first been opened in the 1960s. This trench was only 30 metres from the Heel Stone, the huge monolith that marks the final approach to the Stones (and which visitors pass close by as they complete their circuit of the monument). The earlier dig had revealed that the chalk at the bottom of the trench had been fissured by a number of close,

An aerial photograph showing the re-excavation of a trench that had been first opened in the 1960s, across the Avenue from the Heel Stone.

parallel-running ridges, which superficially resembled plough marks or wheel ruts, but which on re-excavation proved to be far too deep (50 centimetres or 18 inches) and wide (30 centimetres or 1 foot). Perhaps they were the remains of numerous temporary wooden fences to channel crowds of visitors or worshippers.

But as soon as the project's two soil scientists examined the ridges, they were in absolutely no doubt: the ridges were entirely natural, the results of erosion when the glacial ice sheets had begun to melt. Such grooves are well known in chalky areas, but these ones had been made much deeper than normal by the freezing and thawing of a large amount of water, channelled in by the undulations of the landscape immediately around them. In other words, these much-enlarged gullies were a very localized phenomenon. But there was another important point. Normally features within the sub-soil cannot be seen on the surface, but both soil scientists were agreed that the size of the gullies would have made them highly visible in the centuries after the Ice Age, when the thick topsoil that conceals them from modern view would not yet have accumulated. Put another way, the gullies and ridges would have been a striking feature of the area at the time those huge posts were erected in what later was to become the car park.

The excavation went on to prove that the ditches and the slight banks that defined the first, northeasterly length of the much later Avenue were essentially a natural feature, caused by erosion along a gully.[15] It just so happened that this gully was precisely aligned on the solstice. Indeed, the precision of the two alignments (the natural feature and the Avenue) was far too close to be coincidental. And of course the inescapable conclusion was that the direction of sunrise and sunset at the two annual solstices must have been significant to the hunters of early Mesolithic times – just as it was to the constructors of the Avenue, over five thousand years later. It was now clear why this particular spot had been chosen by the people who erected the huge posts in the car park. But were the natural gullies the only reason why people came to the area such a long time ago?

We saw earlier that it used to be believed that in the five millennia prior to the arrival of farming people lived shifting and somewhat impoverished lives. Excavations at sites like Star Carr, however, have clearly shown that this was not the case. It was also believed that burials took place without ceremony, but again, that has been shown to be untrue. In fact, the first proven Mesolithic burials yet found in England are from a cemetery site at Greylake in Somerset. Most remarkably they are very early too, dating to 8500–8200 BC.[16]

Recent research has suggested that the Mesolithic population around what was later to become Stonehenge was much larger than had previously been supposed. During their examination of a ditch and bank known as the Stonehenge Palisade, the Stonehenge Riverside Project revealed that the Palisade post-dated Stonehenge itself. While the team were removing the topsoil around the Palisade, they discovered large numbers of very characteristic long, blade-like early Mesolithic flint tools, clear evidence of rubbish dropped by the inhabitants of a nearby settlement.[17] What is significant for our story is that this debris was found just 400 metres south of the huge posts in the car park. However, the Mesolithic flints found in the soil over and around the Stonehenge Palisade were not precisely *in situ*. Like so much of the modern landscape of Salisbury Plain, the original position of the flints had been disturbed by agriculture and other later activity; all we can say is that they were lost within this locality. We cannot be more precise. So was this the place where the people who erected the pine posts had actually lived?

Simple questions deserve straight answers, but sometimes life is more complex – especially in the case of Stonehenge, where new discoveries are being made at such an extraordinary rate. A most remarkable new site has recently been revealed by another, smaller project at Blick Mead, just

An example of an
Aurochs skeleton.

1 ¼ miles (2 km) east of Stonehenge, close by the River Avon. Blick Mead is located on low-lying land just outside an Iron Age enclosure known as Vespasian's Camp, but this location is entirely coincidental, as the site that concerns us is some seven millennia earlier than the camp.[18]

Blick Mead was carefully chosen by a team led by David Jacques who was seeking a site where preservation was good. Much of Vespasian's Camp had been disturbed by landscaping in the eighteenth century. Modern house-building had also affected other areas, but the low-lying, flood-prone land, by a spring near the river in a meadow called Blick Mead, seemed to have escaped damage. And this was demonstrated during the first season of excavation in 2005. Subsequently the picture has become richer and more complex. In essence, the deposits at Blick Mead consist of finds of Mesolithic settlement debris that has accumulated around a large freshwater spring. But unlike the finds from around the Stonehenge Palisade, these ones were still in their original positions. The debris consists mostly of tens of thousands of flint fragments, but there are also large quantities of animal bone – the remains of meals, to judge from the clear cuts and scratches left by butchering.

The debris found at Blick Mead includes the largest collection of wild cattle (known as aurochs) bones yet found on a British Mesolithic site. These huge animals – almost twice the size of domestic cattle – are very difficult to hunt and yet there are abundant indications that they were killed and consumed in huge quantities. Red deer and wild boar were also hunted and there are signs that salmon were caught, presumably in the nearby river. It is hard to be precise, but taken together, the evidence suggests that feasting regularly took place near the spring. We will discuss the role of springs in the spiritual lives of prehistoric people in the next chapter, but the muds around the Blick Mead spring also had the unusual property of permanently staining flints and other materials a 'bright magenta pink'.[19] This must surely have seemed magical to people at the time.

Blick Mead has been described as a 'persistent place' – where people frequently returned to settle for longer or shorter periods. We can now assert this with some assurance because a series of radiocarbon dates, taken from undisturbed deposits, show that the site was occupied repeatedly for some three thousand years, starting shortly after 8000 BC (7593–7569 BC). The most recent date span is 4798–4722 BC.[20] This is the longest proven occupation of a British Mesolithic site. The dates prove the area around the spring was occupied at the same time the posts were erected in the car park. Environmental samples suggest that the landscape between Blick Mead and the huge pine posts, just over a mile (1.8 km) to the west, was open and largely treeless. This is ideal hunting country for large beasts, as indeed was the river valley itself. David Jacques has suggested that the pine posts might have served to divert driven wild cattle eastwards, towards the river and its muddy margins, where they could have been killed more readily than on the open, dry ground. Mike Parker Pearson's view was that the pine posts were aligned on Beacon Hill – a prominent feature in the distance – for religious rather than practical reasons. Given what we now know, it seems entirely possible that both explanations are probably correct.

The most recent dates from Blick Mead fall in the centuries immediately prior to the arrival of farming. Although there is still an apparent chronological gap of five to seven centuries at the start of the Neolithic, it is now looking increasingly likely that the Stonehenge landscape was occupied continuously between the erection of the car park posts and the first construction work at Stonehenge itself. This also implies that the sacred nature of that particular landscape could have become a fundamental part of people's belief systems, and not just locally, but probably over a wide area of southern Britain. Although much of this is still speculative, we must not think of these beliefs as being static. Like the sites they gave rise to, they would have continued to evolve.

In the next chapter we will consider the evolution of complex religious and ceremonial landscapes, following the arrival of farming in the area shortly after 4000 BC. But we must recall that these developments, spectacular as they were, had roots that extended back three thousand years. It is now apparent that some of the complexity visible in the later ceremonial landscapes of the Neolithic and Bronze Ages had Mesolithic origins. But there was a big difference too – the hunter-forager communities of the Mesolithic revered certain natural features, such as the Blick Mead spring, or the sub-soil gullies beneath the later Avenue. They did not feel it necessary, or perhaps even respectful, to enhance these natural places in any way (although the pine posts are an obvious exception, perhaps emphasizing the unique status of the area). All of that, however, was to change in the centuries after 4000 BC and the arrival of farming. By this time, communities had the manpower, technology and confidence to make more permanent marks on the landscape, in the form of ditches, mounds, banks and, latterly, of standing stones. And this work was to take place with extraordinary frequency and gathering momentum. The pace of our story is starting to hot up.

[overleaf]
*Stonehenge at Twilight, c.*1840
by William Turner
(1789–1862).

2

THE STONEHENGE
'RITUAL LANDSCAPE'
[4000–1500 BC]

The arrival of farming and its rapid adoption by the British population had a profound effect on the societies involved. Within two or three centuries these societies were constructing burial mounds and erecting ceremonial monuments where people – probably from different communities – would gather together. As time passed, farms and larger settlements came into being, but because these were never intended to leave permanent marks on the landscape, they are archaeologically much harder to detect.

Archaeologists, and antiquarians before them, had long recognized that prehistoric burial mounds and ceremonial monuments rarely occurred on their own. Indeed, I well recall working on a very strange site, known as Seahenge, on the beach at Holme-next-the-Sea in Norfolk.[21] It consisted of an upside-down oak tree – whose spreading roots resembled branches – surrounded by a ring-wall of large oak posts. But this shrine was tiny: just six metres across – you could have fitted dozens of Seahenges within Stonehenge. Interestingly, the tiny enclosed space around the oak tree was entered by a deliberately narrow, restricted entranceway, which faced southwest, once again on that solsticial alignment – but this time towards the midwinter sunset.[22] Most remarkably of all, Seahenge could be precisely dated by tree-rings to the months of April–June in the year 2049 BC. At the time it was excavated everybody believed it was an isolated find, being located just above the low-tide line on a remote North Sea foreshore. And then a few months later, the sea revealed another timber circle, about a hundred yards further along the beach.[23] This time the site was a barrow or burial mound, whose ancient timbers produced a date that was identical to the first Seahenge. Doubtless future tides will reveal further sites.

This tendency for prehistoric religious and funerary sites to occur in groups has led British prehistorians to describe them as belonging to so-called 'ritual landscapes'. As we saw in the previous chapter, 'ritual' is the term that prehistorians use to describe all aspects of religion, belief and ideology. Ritual landscapes can be quite small, as I suspect the Seahenge group on the Norfolk coast will prove to be; alternatively, they can be huge and complex. The Stonehenge ritual landscape is vast and contains many smaller sub-landscapes within it, which can be defined in various ways; for example, by time or by types of monument. Nowadays computers with GIS (Geographic Information Systems) are used to map the complexities of 'viewsheds' or the visibility of various monuments, both to and from each other, within complex ritual landscapes.[24] This is a particularly useful approach in undulating landscapes, such as Salisbury Plain.

Being in an area that has been ploughed, but has not been subjected to the sort of deep and intensive farming that has happened elsewhere in lowland Britain, the Stonehenge ritual landscape is remarkably well preserved. But it is far from unique. There is a huge and equally well-preserved ritual landscape some 20 miles (32 km) to the north around the village and stone circle of Avebury. This major complex includes Silbury Hill, the largest man-made artificial mound in prehistoric Europe. Well-preserved ritual landscapes abound outside Wessex in the Orkney Islands, on the River Boyne in Ireland and in upland areas of Wales, Cornwall, northern England and Scotland.[25]

The arrival of aerial survey in the first half of the twentieth century revealed that there had once been enormous ritual landscapes in the intensively farmed areas of lowland Britain, too.[26] Some in the Thames Valley, for example, are of comparable size to that around Stonehenge. The big difference is that many of the lowland monuments used wood in their construction. Over time, these timbers rotted, and allowed later farmers to cut into the mounds and banks with their ploughs. Today all that remains are marks in the soil and only deep features, such as graves, survive at all intact.

The ritual landscapes of Britain did not grow haphazardly. Some, such as the landscape around Stonehenge, can be shown to be very ancient indeed, but others seem to have come into existence in the centuries after the arrival of farming in 4000 BC. Quite a few are even later, with origins around

2500 BC, at the start of the Bronze Age. Quite a high proportion of the
known ritual landscapes seem to have been positioned close by special places
that would have been revered in prehistoric times.[27] These included
waterfalls, spectacular outcrops of rock or high cliffs, but subtler features
could prove attractive too, such as islands in lakes and rivers, or natural
springs, as we saw at Blick Mead. And as we now know from the Stonehenge
Avenue, very subtle features indeed, such as those parallel deep gullies, could
also be treated with reverence.

The Stonehenge gullies provide a further hint as to why such landscape
features were regarded as special. We have known for some time that
people have always regarded spectacular features in the world's landscapes
as carrying particular significance. Ayers Rock, or Uluru, in Australia is a
good example. This holy place is regarded with great reverence by the
indigenous Aboriginal people not just as a ceremonial shrine, but as an
example of the powers that shaped, and still order, their lives. The
profound resonance of such places is hard for Western minds to grasp.
They illustrate and demonstrate man's place in the universe. They demand
respect and humility because they also symbolize the structure that under-
lies all aspects of family life and social organization. At sunrise and sunset
they represent the passage of time and links to the afterlife and the realm
of the ancestors.

Among less spectacular natural features of the landscape, springs offer
glimpses into spirit worlds beneath the ground. Water has long been
recognized as having particular symbolic significance. In a world before
mirrors, the surface of tranquil water reflected the reality of an individual's
appearance; at the same time it sustained life, by quenching thirst. It also
symbolized purity and cleanliness. Many world religions feature forms of
baptism involving washing in water. But it could also symbolize death –
through drowning. In pre-scientific times such mystical places afforded
people a focus for their spiritual and social lives. Their significance cannot be
overestimated. Indeed, their profundity explains why such places continued

THE RITUAL LANDSCAPE

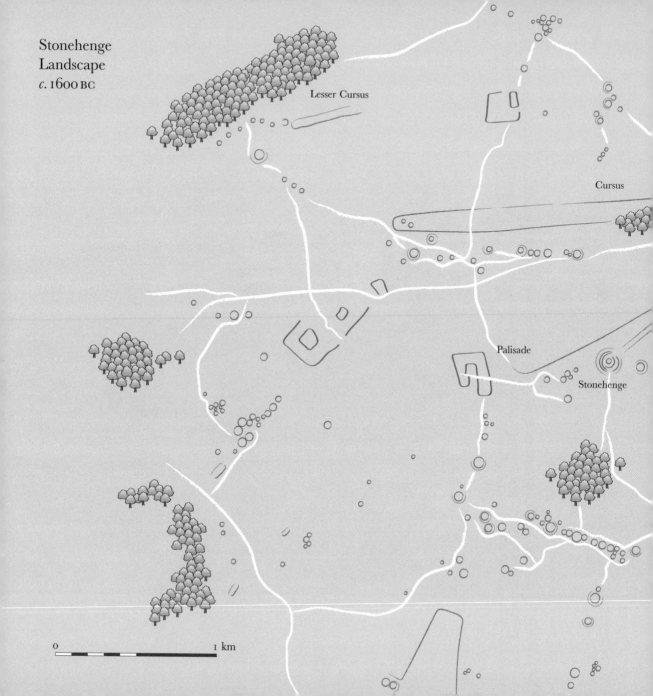

Stonehenge
Landscape
c. 1600 BC

Lesser Cursus

Cursus

Palisade

Stonehenge

0   1 km

Durrington Walls

Woodhenge

Cuckoo Stone

Amesbury 42
Long Barrow

Avenue

Coneybury

River Avon

Bluestonehenge

N

to be revered for millennia. And the complexity of the ritual landscapes that eventually grew up around them reflects the many aspects and dimensions of contemporary religious beliefs.

The term 'ritual landscape' is used to describe areas where burial mounds and a variety of ceremonial sites occur together. The individual sites nearly always respect each other's existence: in other words, later burial mounds are rarely built over earlier ones. Very often, too, we can detect evidence of a wider scheme of organization: burial mounds, for example, are often arranged in rows, along ridge-tops or hillsides. Were these the last resting places of different families or dynasties – the equivalent of family plots in country churchyards of the eighteenth and nineteenth centuries? We will look at the variety of monument-types found in ritual landscapes shortly, but here we need to note only that the earliest barrows and ceremonial monuments we know about were constructed from about 3800 BC – two or three centuries after the arrival of the first Neolithic farmers just before 4000 BC. They then grew in size and complexity throughout the Neolithic and the first half of the Bronze Age, coming to an end, quite abruptly, sometime around 1500 BC. We will discuss their rapid decline in Chapter 8.

Most prehistorians agree that the monuments found in ritual landscapes served to keep distant communities together. Today we are used to meeting long-lost friends and relatives at life's important 'rites of passage', such as baptisms, graduations, marriages and funerals. But such meetings were even more important in prehistory when communities were geographically further apart and travelling was less straightforward. In prehistory, just as today, these gatherings served more than the single purpose for which people were invited. So young people would meet new suitors at funerals and older folk could choose who was going to inherit their estates at marriages or baptisms. Farmers could agree livestock deals at any event they chose to attend. And there were probably gatherings, too, which were not organized by the family or the tribe. Very often these would take place at monuments erected on the edges of tribal territories. In lowland areas of Britain, ritual landscapes are frequently located along the floodplains of major rivers.[28] Rivers often formed tribal boundaries and sites positioned along their floodplains could be seen as neutral – as was the higher ground around lower-lying or more fertile landscapes. Salisbury Plain was probably just such an area.

The first good evidence for the use of the Stonehenge area in Neolithic times does not come in the form of a tomb, as might be expected. In fact, like so many of the recent revelations on Stonehenge's use and early history, it was revealed by archaeologists carrying out research. Between 1980 and 1986 Julian Richards directed the Stonehenge Environs Project, which featured intensive survey (collecting flints, etc. from the surface), combined with selected excavation. The results, published in 1990, still form the basis for all current research into the Stones and their surrounding landscape.[29] During the second season of excavation at the Coneybury Henge, some 600 metres west of the Stonehenge Avenue, the team came upon a large pit a few paces northwest of the henge,[30] which had been dug and then filled with the debris of feasting. The size of the meal was extraordinary: at least ten cattle, some seven roe deer, a red deer and one pig had been slaughtered and butchered. The sheer scale of the feasting strongly recalls the evidence of much earlier celebrations at Blick Mead.

After the feast, or feasts, the bones were carefully buried in the pit, together with hundreds of pieces of early Neolithic pottery and flint tools. Material from the pit has given radiocarbon dates that range around 3800–3700 BC. This spread quite neatly bridges the gap between the final dates at Blick Mead and the Formative Stage at Stonehenge, around 3300 BC, which is discussed further in the next chapter. It also proves beyond any doubt that at the start of the Neolithic period, this part of Salisbury Plain was being used for ritual purposes on a very large scale indeed. More to the point, the pit at Coneybury is unlikely to prove a one-off find; given the hundreds of monuments that occur across the Stonehenge ritual landscape,

we can safely assume that many more pits of this size and age are waiting to be discovered.[31]

The earliest tombs of the Neolithic were communal. Chambers for the dead could be made from stone slabs, drystone walling or timber. The chambers were covered by a long trapezoidal mound, which was modelled on the shape of earlier Neolithic houses on the continent. The soil, turf and rock used to form the mound were quarried from ditches that ran the length of both long sides. Most of these so-called long barrows were entered from a short corridor that reached into the barrow from the widest and highest point of the mound, which was located at one end. Very often the wide end of the long barrow was walled and marked out by slabs and paving to form a forecourt. The forecourt was where funeral ceremonies took place. The body, or the bones, were then carried along the corridor to the appropriate side-chamber. Most probably these were arranged family by family. But unlike modern burials, the bodies were not allowed to rest for eternity. Indeed, there is abundant evidence that bones were regularly removed, most probably for ceremonies that required the presence of an ancestor. Frequently the bones were not returned to the correct body – and became muddled with others. One of the best preserved of these tombs is the West Kennet Long Barrow, some 20 miles to the north of Stonehenge. It formed part of the Avebury ritual landscape.

The Stonehenge area is known to have included some fifteen long barrows, of which ten could be said to have been located within the ritual landscape that was centred on the Stones but none has been the subject of extensive modern excavation.[32] The earliest radiocarbon dates obtained from samples in quarry ditches are no older than about 3600 BC. This is about two centuries later than the earliest known long barrows elsewhere in England.

Then, from about 3500 BC we see a shift away from communal tombs. At first this happens in long barrows and a few round barrows, but after about 2400 BC (during the British Chalcolithic) smaller, round barrows rapidly gain

The forecourt at Wayland's Smithy, on the Ridgeway in Oxfordshire.

The excavation of the
enclosure ditch, with
offerings still in place, at
Etton in the Welland Valley,
near Peterborough.

in popularity. These sites lack the distinctive forecourt and feature a primary burial at the centre, which was often accompanied by expensive grave goods, such as flint, then later copper or bronze daggers. But unlike the earlier communal burials, these bodies had all been placed permanently to rest, sometimes in coffins, in sealed mounds of earth or rubble. Rubble mounds, popular in upland areas, are known as cairns. This change in burial practice is quite profound and is generally taken to indicate that the upper echelons of tribal society were becoming more hierarchical. A formalized class system was beginning to develop.

If barrows were the focus of family or clan attention, other classes of monument were created to appeal to a wider audience. The earliest of these are the 'causewayed enclosures', which were in use between about 3800–3500 BC. This rather unimaginative name is, however, an accurate description. These sites consist of one or more ditches surrounding an irregular but more or less oval, or circular, area. The ditches are dug in variable lengths, maybe 10 or 20 metres long, each one of which is separated from the next by a gap, or causeway. The banks of upcast from the ditches tend to be irregular, but are often placed on the internal side of the ditch. Their construction must have taken much labour.

In the mid-1980s I was able to excavate an exceptionally well-preserved causewayed enclosure at Etton, in the Welland Valley on the western Fen margins near Peterborough, a site that will be discussed further in Appendix II.[33] The ditch was waterlogged and had preserved wood, bark and other organic remains – such as the earliest piece of string (made from flax) yet found in Britain. Close examination revealed that the ditch (which had been opened in 3725–3670 BC) had been dug and then immediately filled with offerings, which were placed along the bottom in neatly defined heaps.[34] These offerings consisted of human skulls, or inverted pots, whose round bases closely resembled skulls. Some of the offerings were of meat bones, or dog skulls. In one case an inverted pot had been placed on a birch bark mat. In a few places querns, or corn-

THE RITUAL LANDSCAPE

grinding stones, had been deliberately broken, before being offered to the ground. Taken together there seemed little doubt that the offerings were often the remains of feasting and were making statements about domestic or family life.

We soon reached the conclusion that the material placed in each length of ditch represented people or events in a particular family's history. We cannot be certain that this would have been the case in all causewayed enclosures right across Britain; finds in causewayed enclosures in the southwest and Cornwall, for example, seem to suggest a focus on warfare as well as domestic life. But the primacy of the family, clan and tribe in the organization of these particular monuments surely signifies something of fundamental importance to the development of later monuments in ritual landscapes. Visitors to Stonehenge also often visit Avebury, a short drive to the north. Here they can visit Windmill Hill, probably the most famous causewayed enclosure in Britain.[35]

The Stonehenge landscape includes just one complete causewayed enclosure, known as Robin Hood's Ball, about 4 miles (6.5 km) to the northwest of the Stones.[36] Although it has not yielded many radiocarbon samples, it appears to have been constructed around 3600 BC.[37] In common with sites like Etton, its ditches produced evidence of feasting and disarticulated human bones. The disarticulation of the human bones provides a link to the way bodies or loose bones were often removed from the chambers of contemporary long barrows to attend ceremonies that required the 'participation' of the ancestors. Maybe causewayed enclosures were where these rites took place – with, as might be expected, feasting.

Although we know about only one *bona fide* causewayed enclosure in the area, the earliest feature of what was to develop into Stonehenge was the circular ditch that surrounds the site and which can still be seen as a slight depression in the mown grass. We will discuss this ditch in Chapter 3 and in Appendix II, but it was not dug in one single operation, like, for example, most contemporary round barrow quarry ditches. Its shape is slightly

An aerial photograph of Stonehenge showing the circular ditch which surrounds the site.

The Cursus barrows at
Stonehenge.

irregular and it is accompanied by an internal bank – both features of causewayed enclosures.

We saw earlier that sometime around 3500 BC single, central burials, probably of important people, are found beneath long barrows and increasingly below round barrows. This is also the approximate date when we begin to come across strange monuments formed of two parallel ditches that from the air resemble old airfield runways. They were once believed to have been the sites of special or sacred races, hence their name *cursus* (the Latin word for a race course). They are a very variable class of monument, but they consist of two long parallel ditches with banks on the inside. By far the longest is the famous Dorset Cursus in Cranborne Chase,which is 6¼ miles (10 km) long. At Stonehenge the Greater Cursus runs for 1¾ miles (2.8 km) and is about 150 metres-wide. It can be clearly seen by visitors walking between the Visitor Centre and the Stones. The east end of the cursus is aligned on a contemporary long barrow, which probably formed a part of the monument complex. A much smaller cursus, the Lesser Cursus, was constructed some 600 metres (655 yd) northwest of the western end of the Greater Cursus.[38] In the landscape around Stonehenge, as on Cranborne Chase later, the positioning of Bronze Age barrows clearly respects the layout and orientation of the two cursuses, which suggests that like other early features of the ritual landscape they continued to play a part in the positioning of new sites in the area.

However, the best-known type of monument to be found in ritual landscapes is undoubtedly the henge. Named after Stonehenge, henges are only found in Britain and Ireland. They consist of a circular ditch with an external bank and one or more entranceways. Very often they surround rings of standing stones or large timbers. Incidentally, neither Stonehenge nor Seahenge are henges, if you follow this definition rigidly: the ditch at the former has an internal bank and the latter lacks a ditch entirely. Stonehenge is generally grouped with other early henges under the general heading of 'formative henges', which were constructed around 3200–2800 BC. Very often

THE RITUAL LANDSCAPE

these early henges are associated with burials – as indeed was the case at Stonehenge (see Chapter 4).

Frequently large henges are linked to other elements of the ritual landscape by alignments, or alternatively by processional ways of some sort. At Etton, for example, the causewayed enclosure was linked to the large Maxey henge by the Maxey Cursus. At Avebury the great henge is approached by the West Kennet and more recently discovered Beckhampton Avenues.[39] In the Stonehenge landscape the principal axis seems to have been formed by the later Avenue (see Chapter 6), which, as we have seen, follows the solsticial alignment of the grooves in the underlying bedrock. Today, on every summer solstice, public and media attention focuses on the sunrise approach to the Stones, from the northeast. But it should not be forgotten that the solsticial alignment continues in a straight line to the southwest, the direction of midwinter sunset. If you continue along this alignment towards the southwest, soon you will encounter a low ridge that runs roughly east–west and forms the southern horizon or 'viewshed' of the Stonehenge basin. This was perhaps the prime viewing point for the Stones. And of course it was reached by following the line of the solstice.

All ritual landscapes feature large numbers of Bronze Age round barrows, many of which can be dated to the centuries on either side of 2000 BC. These were the equivalent of graves in a churchyard, although often additional burials would be inserted into the mound, as so-called 'secondaries', at a somewhat later date. I have never counted the number of barrows around Stonehenge, but in the first two decades of the nineteenth century two archaeologists excavated some 200 between them! The importance of the Stonehenge landscape is reflected in the richness of some of the burials placed within round barrows. But this brings us back to that prime viewing point, along the southern edge of the Stonehenge basin.

Today this ridge is known as Normanton Down and it includes a group of barrows, arranged as a series of humps along the top of the ridge. When excavated, some of these produced some extraordinarily rich grave goods.

These barrows date to the final stages of the ritual landscape's development and recent research suggests that the people who were buried in them might have played an important part in controlling access to Stonehenge in its final years.[40] We will discuss these barrows further in Chapter 7.

Archaeology is essentially a practical approach to the past. Its great strength lies in the way places in the landscape – mounds, stones and rocks – can be explained by new ideas. Through the archaeologist's knowledge and imagination, inanimate objects may be given new life. And that is precisely what has happened quite recently at Stonehenge. In the following chapters we will see how a simple but vivid idea has transformed our appreciation of the way the Stones, and the ritual landscape that surrounds them, might have been understood by the thousands of people who came there, from Britain and even further afield, every year. If this theory is correct, then Stonehenge and the ritual landscape that still surrounds it was all about the transition from life to death. Surely, nothing could be more important.

[overleaf]
Sheep Grazing at Stonehenge
by William Turner
(1789–1862).

3

BEFORE THE GREAT STONES, PART I: THE FORMATIVE STAGE

[FROM 3300 BC]

Shortly before 4000 BC the first farmers arrived in Britain, bringing with them a more settled way of life. It used to be believed that this shift to food production had been achieved by a massive invasion involving complete population change, but recent DNA evidence suggests that the ratio of new arrivals to natives was in the range 1:3 to 1:4.[41] This would explain why earlier Mesolithic sacred landscapes continued to be important into Neolithic times. But it would be a huge mistake to believe that the rites and ceremonies practised at the various shrines, in what were now rapidly developing ritual landscapes, owed much at all to earlier forms of belief. We now understand that the Neolithic was a time of rapid social, economic and intellectual development. People were thinking about their lives and their surroundings in new and very different ways.

In the previous chapter we saw how the earliest Neolithic sites in the Stonehenge landscape were at some distance from the Stones, although this is almost certainly due to the fact that most of these were chance or haphazard discoveries. The earliest find was the pit near Coneybury Henge, which was dug in the two centuries after 4000 BC. Other sites included a number of long barrows, the Greater and the Lesser Cursuses and Robin Hood's Ball, the causewayed enclosure north of Stonehenge.

In the actual area to be occupied by the Stones, the earliest feature to be constructed was the enclosing circular ditch, with an intermittent bank on either side. Today the ditch has become almost entirely filled in, but it can still be seen as a shallow depression marked by two very low banks. We now know that these surface marks are a very pale reflection of what still lies below the surface. We do not know precisely when the ditch was first dug, but work probably began sometime around 3300 BC. The digging of the ditch, which probably took place over an extended period, is here taken as the start point for the initial or Formative Stage of Stonehenge, which seems to have come to an end around, or just before, 2900 BC.

The diameter of the ditch is approximately 118 metres (385 ft). When open, it would have been about 2 metres (6.5 ft) deep, and roughly twice as wide. It was positioned on the axis of the natural subsoil ridges that were aligned on the solstice – although by this period they would not have been apparent from the surface.

In addition to an intermittent ditch and bank, a further feature common to both the Stonehenge ditch and causewayed enclosure ditches is their repeated digging out and filling in. This process seems to have been a part of their use as shrines, where offerings were placed in the ground and were covered over with soil. It is suggested in Appendix II that the ditch at Stonehenge was dug and recut in much the same way, although several centuries later. Photographs of the material filling the ditch, which were taken during the excavations in the 1920s, show the mixing of layers that was so characteristic at Etton.[42] Layers where soils were able to form are infrequent, as are places where the sides of the ditch have washed in. These are all natural processes that one would expect to encounter if the ditch had simply been dug and then abandoned to silt-up naturally.

There was also evidence that some offerings had been disturbed, and the highly irregular pit-like shape of the ditch suggests that its original digging was essentially a process of gradual extension and enlargement – both practices that recall what happened earlier at causewayed enclosures. Unfortunately the evidence for this possible early digging of the ditch was not recognized when roughly half was removed during large-scale excavations in the 1920s, directed by Lt.-Col. William Hawley. Furthermore, the last recutting of the ditch, which took place in Stage 1 (Chapter 5), also seems to have been very thorough, especially around the main entrance-way, and may well have removed much evidence for the ditch's original digging and primary use. For these reasons we still cannot be certain when the ditch was first dug, but it is very unlikely to have been before 3500 BC. Taken together, the available evidence suggests that activity within the area enclosed by the ditch began around 3300 BC. So the ditch must have been in existence at least by then – although an earlier date for its initial opening cannot be ruled out.

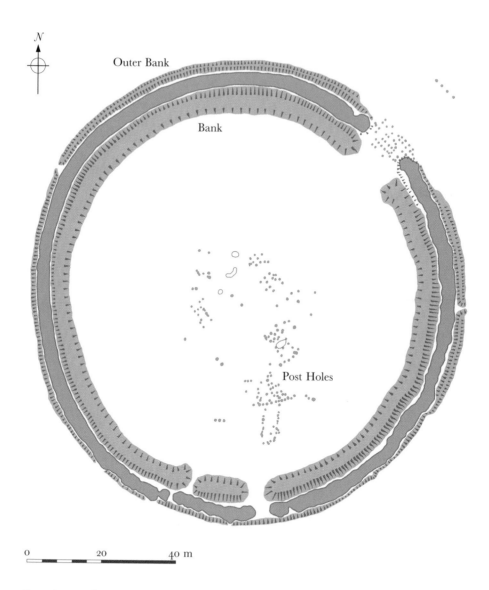

N

Outer Bank

Bank

Post Holes

0   20   40 m

Stonehenge, Stage 1 *c.*2900 BC

At first, the ditch itself may have been the focus for ceremonies, but soon the land it enclosed became increasingly important. It is still not generally appreciated, but Stonehenge was one of the largest cremation cemeteries in Neolithic Europe. It was by far the biggest in Britain, with 63 known cremations, and probably about 150 in all. At least three of these cremations have given radiocarbon dates that range between 3300 and 2900 BC (see Appendix II). The problem, however, with dating cremations is that they could have been old ones, brought to Stonehenge from somewhere else. Rather strangely, the arrangement of the few known cremation findspots does not appear to form a coherent pattern, but this reflects the fact that Hawley failed to record their precise location in his general trenches across the interior. Subsequent research suggests that many cremations were found towards the southern ditch entranceway and around the inner ditch bank and the encircling Aubrey Holes.* Recent re-excavation of Aubrey Hole 7 revealed a cremation directly alongside it which Hawley had failed to spot in the 1920s. This cremation has given a radiocarbon date of 3039–2900 BC.[43]

In addition to cremations, the area enclosed by the ditch also includes numerous post-holes, which do not appear to form any obvious circular pattern that might possibly anticipate the later Stones. Some of the central post holes are massive and there are hints, if anything, of rectangular structures.[44] One set of posts traverse the main entranceway in four or five slightly haphazard rows, which might have included two deliberately restricted entranceways.[45] The soil filling the post-holes did not contain fragments chipped off the later stones during their shaping, as were found in the holes that held the upright stones. This suggests that the posts pre-date the main use of the site. The positioning of the posts across the main entranceway suggests that the ditch was in existence when they were erected. At least one of the larger posts in the central group of post-holes had rotted in place, as its outline or 'ghost' survived as a stain in the soil.[46] It was a large

---

* For an explanation of the holes, and their name, see page 91.

An early medieval
interpretation of the
construction of Stonehenge.

post, although not quite as substantial as the Mesolithic pines in the car park (Chapter 2).

A rather intriguing arrangement of posts was noted by Hawley in his excavations in the 1920s. He called it the 'Passageway' and he believed it to have been roofed – although this seems unlikely, as the posts on either side do not form pairs.[47] The Passageway is, however, clearly lined up on the southern entranceway. The size and position of the Stonehenge Passageway is quite closely matched by a timber 'gateway', which is also aligned on an entranceway, at Etton.[48] Stone and wooden entrance structures are known at other causewayed enclosures. Maybe the Stonehenge Passageway is a later variant of an already well-established tradition.

There are hints at other post-built screens and structures in the large number of post-holes that we know about. Doubtless many were not recorded in the earlier excavations and doubtless, too, many were destroyed in prehistory, during the erection of the main stone settings. The sheer numbers and the proliferation of fragmentary patterns of post-holes suggest that the Formative Stage of the site was extended and might well have lasted for more than just two or three centuries.

It also seems probable that a few standing stones were erected at this early stage in Stonehenge's development. Stone-holes have been found towards the centre of the site, one of which appears to form the focus of a ring of post-holes. The size of these stone-holes suggests they were probably dug to receive stones of the local sarsen sandstone, which may well have been lying on the surface nearby since the Ice Age. The huge, and unshaped Heel Stone (a name it acquired in the seventeenth century), which stands just outside the main entranceway, may also have been erected at this very early stage.

The use of Stonehenge in its Formative Stage was certainly never unstructured nor haphazard. For a start, it took place both within the ditch and the area it enclosed. And although the digging of the ditch was most probably community-based gang work, its size and overall plan had been

agreed before construction began. Similarly, subsequent redigging took place within the confines of the ditch and its external banks. It is also unlikely that the distribution of cremations across the interior was entirely at random. We have seen that there is evidence to suggest that most cremations were buried closer to the ditch and its internal bank. This is significant because it is entirely consistent with what was observed at Etton and other causewayed enclosures, where small pits, filled with offerings, tended to cluster around individual ditch segments.[49] If the ditch segments at causewayed enclosures were indeed controlled by different families or kin groups, as seems most probable, then the small pits with offerings represent significant events in the lives of individual members of that kin group. At Stonehenge, some 500 years later, that tradition was continued but with cremations placed in the small pits. We will most probably never understand why the many posts were erected across the interior, but the Passageway structure, aligned as it is on the southern entranceway, does suggest that the cremations were indeed buried with some ceremony.

There is also evidence to suggest that even in its earliest phase Stonehenge and the features within it were based on solar and astronomical alignments, although these were never as precise as what was to happen later.[50] The most obvious example being, of course, the northeast-facing main entranceway.

So to sum up: the digging of the ditch, the creation of a huge cremation cemetery and the building of numerous structures from wooden posts suggest that Stonehenge was being used by large groups of people, and most probably for a long time, before there is clear evidence for the construction of more coherent, stone-built structures. Much of this use, like that of causewayed enclosures several centuries earlier, would have been episodic and most probably happened during the quieter times of the farming year, such as autumn or late spring. We currently believe that this early work probably began around 3300 BC, although the ditch could have been dug slightly earlier. Then, in the years around 3000 BC, there was a major change towards more centralized, more concerted construction. It would seem that individual communities had begun to co-operate more closely. This social integration would become a process that would gradually gain in strength for the next 1500 years. And it would not just happen at Stonehenge.

Great henges within ritual landscapes were being constructed right across the British Isles. But the people constructing and altering these new shrines were not doing pointless work. Certainly the great structures they bequeathed us are remarkable, even awe-inspiring to look at, but they should be seen for what they actually achieved. It was the coming together to construct, change and rebuild these sites that enabled communities to work together and cement increasingly strong local ties. It would inevitably have led to better infrastructure and would have helped to shape and reinforce a huge variety of social and practical networks. From 3000 BC there is increasing evidence – for example, in pottery styles and monument form – that regional identities were becoming more firmly established.[51] Neither Stonehenge nor prehistoric British societies would ever be the same again.

[overleaf]
Stonehenge, 1981
by John Piper (1903–1992).

4

BEFORE THE GREAT STONES, PART II: STAGE 1
[FROM 3000 BC]

Before we go any further we should define more closely what we mean by the term 'Great Stones'. These are the huge, grey sandstone blocks that form the main uprights and lintels at Stonehenge. The stone used is known as sarsen (a word whose origins imply 'heathen' or 'pagan').* It occurs widely near the surface across Salisbury Plain and the Marlborough Downs and consists of a silicified (i.e. cemented by silica) sandstone that is extremely hard and durable once it has been exposed to the elements. When freshly quarried it is more pink in colour and much easier to shape. The largest sarsens at Stonehenge weigh around 50 tonnes. These huge stones should not be confused with the very much smaller (2–4 tonnes) bluestones, which, as we will see shortly, were transported to Stonehenge from Wales; they acquired their name because of their colour when freshly quarried or chipped. Today, all the stones at Stonehenge have much the same greyish appearance (the bluestones perhaps slightly darker), especially when seen from a distance.

The ready availability of sarsen so close to the surface must help explain why the so-called megalithic monuments, such as Stonehenge and Avebury, were quite so massive. The word megalith was first used in the mid-nineteenth century and derives from two Greek words meaning 'large' and 'stone' and in the past was even used to describe Megalithic people, cultures or the Megalithic Age. The term is used less often today, because the movement and shaping of large stones is seen as something that a variety of quite dissimilar local communities wanted to do in order to create enduring tombs and monuments. Put another way, it was a local response to a readily available resource. It is hard to imagine, as one drives through the rolling Wiltshire countryside, that the neatly laid-out fields of wheat and barley would once have been covered with large and small sarsen stones, left stranded on the surface by the movement of Ice Age glaciers.

* The word 'sarsen' derives from 'Saracen', a term that in the Middle Ages implied heathen.

Most of the surface sarsens were removed by farmers and by people looking for stone for building walls, barns and houses. But they do survive in a few places where the land was traditionally grazed and where surface stones would actually have been quite welcome as shelter for sheep in severe winters or during lambing. This helps to explain their local name of 'grey wethers' (wethers are castrated male lambs). A particularly fine group of grey wethers can still be seen lying on the surface around the village of Lockeridge Dene, near Marlborough.[52]

The main local concentration of sarsen stone, both on the surface and in shallow quarries, is in the hills of the Marlborough Downs, around the villages of Avebury and Clatford, some 20 miles north of Stonehenge.[53] Members of the Stonehenge Riverside Project have discovered documentary evidence that in the early eighteenth century large blocks of sarsen lay on the roadside near Clatford, where they had been abandoned, probably on their way to Stonehenge, via Marden (with its famous henge) and down the western side of the valley of the River Avon.[54] It used to be thought that in prehistoric times there were relatively few sarsens lying around on the surface near Stonehenge, but recent research, using the first editions of Ordnance Survey maps (early nineteenth century), has revealed that many are marked, although nearly all have since vanished. At least one stone, near the village and army camp of Bulford, about an hour's walk east of Stonehenge, had been partially shaped and had once been a standing stone.[55]

I have briefly noted that freshly quarried sarsen is easier to shape than stone that has laid on the surface for generations, which becomes extremely hard and very difficult to chip at all. So there would have been good reason to select stone like that from the shallow quarries around Avebury, which had been protected by a covering of earth. The sarsens were given a final dressing when they arrived at Stonehenge. A dense scattering of sarsen chips clearly indicates that most of the shaping of the Great Stones took place to the west of the main entranceway. This would support the idea that the stones were

transported from the north, rather than along the line of the Avenue, as has sometimes been suggested. They were given further shaping as they lay on the ground, radiating out from their pre-dug stone holes, ready to be erected into position. This would explain why their inward face and sides are better and more finely dressed than their outward-facing surfaces, which could only have been shaped once the stone was upright. The shaping was done with sarsen hammer-stones. Experiments have shown that it is best carried out using a ripple-type technique where successive flakes are removed to form parallel shallow rippled grooves. These grooves can be seen quite clearly, especially in low, oblique sunlight. The cruder exterior shaping of the uprights can still be observed by visitors from the modern footpath that skirts around the outside of the Stones. We shall discuss the remarkable revelations of a recent laser scan survey of the Stones' surfaces in the next chapter.

One might reasonably imagine that the builders of the first major stone structure at Stonehenge would have made use of readily available local stone. But that would be to suppose that Stonehenge was constructed for practical purposes with straightforward, business-like motives. But as we have seen, the thoughts and ideas that lay behind it were far more complex.

We now appreciate that there was a more fundamental motive behind the transport of stones over great distances than movement for its own sake. It has been known for some fifty years that polished axes, made from distinctively coloured or patterned stone, were widely distributed across Neolithic Britain. But this distribution was not evenly spread. There were concentrations and voids. Soon most of the quarry sites could be pinned down by geology, often to spectacular upland sites.[56] The uneven distribution showed that certain areas favoured axes from different quarries. Beautiful polished axes from these upland quarries have been found buried in causewayed enclosures and at other special sites, such as barrows. The distinctive greenstone axes found at Etton, the causewayed enclosure we have already discussed, which lies on the edge of the Wash

'Grey wethers' in the village of Lockeridge Dene, near Marlborough.

Fenlands, about 30 miles (50 km) from the North Sea coast, originated high in the Lake District hills, in Cumbria, some 170 miles (275 km) to the northwest. And Etton was not unique: many other sites in the east Midlands have also produced axes from Langdale. So what was going on: was this a simple case of long-distance trade?

Trade in the prehistoric past was very different to its modern equivalent.[57] For a start, money did not exist. Smaller, everyday things would have been exchanged for surplus items at market-like gatherings, which were often positioned at 'neutral' locations on the edges of a tribes or community's territory. Very much later, in the Iron Age, around 500 BC, some of these places would develop into hillforts, and even later, in Roman times, a few would become towns. But valuable, high-status objects were treated differently. These would be passed from one tribal leader or head of a family to another, as symbols, ultimately, of power and influence and friendship. Agreements between community leaders, perhaps after periods of tension, would be sealed with an exchange of such 'gifts' – which of course were nothing of the sort and came with many strings (obligations) attached. Valuable objects, such as the polished greenstone axes from Langdale, which we excavated in some numbers at Etton, acquired greater value and prestige because they were known to have originated in a very special place, far, far away.[58]

The manner in which these high-value objects were treated suggests that some of the mystical properties of the places where they came from were believed to linger with them – rather like the sacred saints' relics of the Christian era. In many tribal societies remote places such as the Langdale quarry, were seen as 'liminal', a word that literally means 'on the edge' (from the Latin *limen*, a threshold). These places and the objects from them were thought to lie at the frontier between our world, the world of the living – and that of the dead – the realm of the ancestors.

We know, thanks to the discovery of a number of tombs and other monuments that the spectacular rocky outcrops of the Preseli Mountains of southwest Wales were probably regarded as special, or liminal, in this way. I have journeyed through these landscapes and they never fail to affect me. The outcrops of rocks can be jagged and spectacular and seem naturally to prefigure or echo the structured order of sites like Stonehenge. I had learnt as a student that since the 1920s geologists had been aware that the distinctive smaller uprights at Stonehenge, known as bluestones, had indeed originated in this part of Wales. Archaeologists had then suggested that the bluestones had been shipped by rafts from coastal quarries in Wales up the Bristol Channel, then eastwards, up the Bristol Avon. After a relatively short overland stretch the stones were then reloaded onto rafts for the journey south along the Wiltshire Avon. The stones were then landed and were ceremonially transported up the Avenue to enter Stonehenge from the northeast, along the line of the midsummer solstice.[59] It was a neat theory, and for the latter part of the twentieth century it seemed to make plenty of sense. But it was probably wrong.

To the general public all the theories about transporting heavy stones over vast distances may have sounded far-fetched (literally), but there were numerous prehistoric examples where huge rocks – some even larger than the largest sarsens at Stonehenge – had been transported long distances. Indeed, it had been known for some time that right across the zone of megalith construction, from Orkney to Brittany, the movement of great rocks was an integral part of their ceremonial construction and use. But almost immediately there were counter-suggestions by geologists that the bluestones had been transported to Wiltshire by Ice Age glaciers.[60] Although they were never accepted by the archaeological profession, these theories found some sympathy with the press and wider public.

More recently, research by the Stonehenge Riverside Project has revealed that some of the specific rock-types that comprise the Stonehenge bluestones come from at least two known quarries on the north side of the Preseli Mountains.[61] This meant that the Bristol Channel sea route to

[overleaf]
The Carn Goedog bluestone quarries, Pembrokeshire. The spectacular location of this quarry and the stark outlines of the bare rocks anticipate the man-made monuments they would eventually form. It is not difficult to see why such places were considered sacred.

England was impossible – or at best highly unlikely. Instead, it made far more sense to have transported the stones overland for the 180-mile (290 -km) journey to Stonehenge. The overland route would also have meant that the movement of the bluestones would have been seen by, and would most probably have involved, people and communities along the route. A modern equivalent would be the carrying of the Olympic Flame around the host nation prior to the Olympic Games. In 2012 it would have made little sense to have sent it around the British Isles by sea! Nobody would have seen it, or been able to run with it.

There has been much speculation on how the large sarsens and the smaller bluestones were moved. Both operations undoubtedly involved large numbers of people, which ultimately, of course, was the purpose behind every project associated with Stonehenge. We must also not forget that people had developed effective techniques for carrying out heavy civil engineering tasks without the use of wheels or pulleys. But we should avoid the temptation of assuming that the stones were necessarily moved in the most efficient way possible. A better example might be the transport of the huge sculpture effigies through the streets of Seville in the annual April Fair, or *Feria*.[62] Here the penitents carry the massive structures on their shoulders; some choose to do this heavy work barefooted and many after fasting. In other words, their purpose was to do the job in a way that was right for them, whatever its practical effectiveness.

Although we do not have space to discuss theories on how the various stones were moved through the landscape, the task would have been made easier if somehow friction could be eased. Water and animal fat can be important lubricants. On a practical note, following the great storm of October 1987 I was offered the opportunity to collect the trunk of a blown-over oak tree from a coastal wood in Suffolk. I was helped by an experienced woodsman who showed me how to move it without mechanical assistance. After removing the roots, the trimmed-up trunk weighed approximately 2 tonnes (the same weight as a large bluestone). First we collected a series of straight wooden rails, made from smaller branches, which we placed, like railway tracks, on the ground. The tree trunk rested on wooden rollers (again made from short lengths of branches), which lay across the rails. On flat surfaces the tree could be pushed by one man, sometimes without the aid of a lever, but even slight gradients required both of us, with levers. Happily for us, the ground where we were working was quite flat, but any gradient worthy of the name would have required large numbers of people, both pushing with levers and pulling with honeysuckle ropes.

Honeysuckle ropes were found at the Early Bronze Age site at Seahenge on the north Norfolk coast.[63] Reconstruction experiments for a *Time Team* television documentary showed that these ropes, made from soaked and twisted honeysuckle stems, were very strong. If sufficient people were available, the central tree trunk (weighing almost 2 tonnes) could simply be dragged, without the use of rails and rollers, especially if the ground surface was wet and a bit slimy. This simple rail and roller system would almost certainly not have worked for the largest sarsen stones, without considerable modification (i.e. multiple rails and/or stone rollers).

The earliest evidence for what one might term concerted action at Stonehenge comes in the form of a series of fifty-six stone holes that are regularly spaced around the inside edge of the inner ditch bank. They are laid out in a circle that has the same centre point as the ditch, which is why both are placed within Stage 1. Of course, sharing a common centre point (which could have been permanently marked in the ground) does not mean that the ditch and the Aubrey Holes were necessarily laid out as part of the same event. Unlike the ditch, the Aubrey Holes form a complete circle, without any apparent entranceways. They were named the Aubrey Holes in honour of John Aubrey, the king's antiquary in the seventeenth century, who drew attention to a number of cavities 'at intervals inside the circular earthwork' (1666).[64] This alerted Lt.-Col. William Hawley, who then

M.r John Aubrey R.S.S. 1666.
Ætat 40:

excavated more than half of them between 1920 and 1924. Hawley's numbering is still used – Aubrey Hole 1 (AH1) is immediately southeast of the Slaughter Stone, which lies at the southeastern side of the main entrance-way; AH 56 lies the same distance to the northwest of the recumbent (lying-down) Slaughter Stone. Hawley excavated all the Aubrey Holes (AH 1–32) in the southeastern half of the circle.

The Aubrey Holes were dug to precisely the right size to receive bluestones of closely similar size to those placed at the centre of the Stones, somewhat later, in Stage 2 (Chapter 5). None of the Aubrey Holes contained bluestones when excavated, but Lt.-Col. William Hawley, who excavated most of the eastern set of holes in the 1920s, noted that the bottom and sides of many had been crushed and compressed, as if a large stone (rather than a post) had been dropped in and later removed (a process that would have required the vertical stone to rocked forwards and backwards to loosen it). Quite often Hawley discovered that cremations had been placed in the Aubrey Holes, and in one instance this had been done after the bluestone had been removed.[65] Mike Parker Pearson has kindly informed me that a radiocarbon date for the insertion of a bluestone into an Aubrey Hole is 3080–2890 BC.[66]

The Stonehenge Riverside Project has investigated two of the bluestone quarry sites that are known to have been worked in the later Neolithic period. The Stonehenge bluestones are essentially of two types: spotted dolerite and various rhyolites, both of which are igneous (volcanic in origin). The rhyolite quarry, at Craig Rhos-y-felin, even revealed a bluestone pillar that had been partially shaped, but abandoned. Radiocarbon dates suggest that this quarry was being worked around 3400–3300 BC, some three or four centuries earlier than the Aubrey Holes.[67] A second quarry, with even closer matches to the Stonehenge spotted dolerite bluestones, was at Carn Goedog. This quarry revealed dressing floors and a built-up earthen ramp down which quarried stones were loaded. This quarry was in use in 3350–3040 BC, again much earlier than the Aubrey Holes.

A portrait of English antiquary and pioneer archaeologist John Aubrey (1626–97). The Aubrey holes at Stonehenge are named after him.

Stage 1 also sees a renewed emphasis on the main northeastern entranceway, which we have seen is aligned on the midsummer sunrise. We have also seen how a band of deep subsoil grooves, just outside the entranceway, follow precisely the same alignment. That alignment must have been significant when the ditch was first laid out, sometime around, or just before 3300 BC. However, the northeastern approach was not the only way into the sacred area, as there was at least one other entranceway to the south. That entranceway, moreover, was approached by a substantial internal timber passageway, most probably constructed in the Formative Stage, as we saw in the previous chapter. But at some time after 3300 BC the southern entranceway becomes of much lesser importance; it is partially blocked and narrowed, but it never goes completely out of use. Indeed, the great Sarsen Circle of Stages 2 and later was broken or interrupted by a smaller, shorter upright (Stone 11) that is never likely to have supported a lintel.[68] In the Styrofoam replica, 'Foamhenge', constructed for television, the experts advising the film-makers suggested that a lighter, timber lintel might have been substituted for stone (see Chapter 9). Rather significantly, this strange break (if that is indeed what it was) in the otherwise complete sarsen circle faces directly across to the southern entranceway.

The re-emphasis of the main northeastern entranceway takes the form of major episodes of recutting the ditch terminals on either side. A line of three stone holes, probably for sarsens, has been found heading northeastwards from the eastern side of the main entranceway. Again, these would have drawn attention to the enhanced entranceway. The emphasis on the entranceway is revealing. Yes, it draws attention to what was happening within the area enclosed by the ditch, its two banks and the new circle of Aubrey Holes, with their bluestones, but it also shifts focus outside and beyond the monument – to the surrounding landscape. It was there – in the final moments of their 2007 excavation – that the Stonehenge Riverside Project made a most extraordinary discovery.[69]

Despite what films and popular accounts might want us to believe, successful archaeologists very rarely stumble on something that is completely unexpected. Nowadays, to run a competent research project requires a series of clearly defined aims and objectives. But these have to be very specific; a pet theory is not enough: it has to be able to be tested on, or in, the ground. In the next chapter I will discuss an innovative idea that originated in the far-off island of Madagascar. When I first read about it, it sounded quite persuasive and I featured it in my book *Britain BC*, as a way of drawing together and explaining the various features of the Stonehenge landscape. Subsequently, however, it has moved on, from being a clever academic concept to something altogether more useful – and of practical importance, because it led, in the last day of the 2007 season, to the discovery of Bluestonehenge. I shall discuss this new site further in the next chapter, but essentially it consisted of a small circle – diameter about 20 metres (65 ft) – of some twenty-five bluestones, which had been positioned directly alongside the River Avon, about 2 ¼ miles (3.5 km), as the crow flies, southeast of the Stones. All the evidence suggests that the stones of Bluestonehenge were placed in the ground at 2950 BC.[70] So it would now seem likely that the stones of Bluestonehenge and the Aubrey Holes were placed in the ground at approximately the same time. But again we must not assume that this was all part of one single event. If the complex archaeology of Stonehenge has taught us anything, it is surely that such assumptions must be demonstrated by excavation.

We will end this chapter with a simple sum that has portents for the future. There were fifty-six bluestones in the Aubrey Holes and about twenty-five at Bluestonehenge – let us call the total from both sites eighty. This is a number we discover again, but in very different circumstances.

[overleaf]
An aquatint of the Grand Conventional Festival of the Britons, published by Robert Havell in 1815.

5

THE GREAT STONES ARRIVE:
STAGE 2
[FROM 2500 BC]

If I had been writing this book thirty years ago, very little of what follows would have been known. The Stonehenge Environs Project (1990), which discovered the Coneybury pit, among many other exciting finds, had set the Stones firmly in their contexts. To add to this, five years later English Heritage published a superb summary of modern excavations of Stonehenge: *Stonehenge in its Landscape: Twentieth-century Excavations*.[71] These two projects provided a solid framework of dates and developments that led to what can only be described as a torrent of new research in the twenty-first century. Thanks to this very recent work we now understand not just when Stonehenge and the sites around it were constructed, but more importantly *why*. The basic groundwork was established by two projects of the 1990s, but something else, some mystery ingredient, was required to put life into what were then mere facts. And that ingredient – I am often tempted to call it magical – was provided by Ramilisonina, an archaeologist from Madagascar, after he had been taken around Stonehenge and Avebury by an English colleague.[72]

Together Mike Parker Pearson and Ramilisonina had been surveying and researching the standing stones and chambered tombs of Madagascar, some of which are still in use today, as part of a continuing tradition among local communities. I can remember when Mike first told me what Ramil (as Ramilisonina is known to his friends) had told him when he first encountered Stonehenge. I am fairly certain it was sometime in 1991 and it has stayed with me ever since, because at the time we were staring down at thousands of Bronze Age timbers, exposed in the wet peats at Flag Fen. I have never been able to look at any ancient wood or timber in quite the same way since. Let me quote Mike's succinct version of Ramil's idea:

> In Madagascar, he explained, people built in stone for the ancestors because stone, like the ancestors, is eternal. Buildings for the living are made of wood because it, like human lives, is transient. Stonehenge was clearly a place for the ancestors.*

---

* Quoted from Mike Parker Pearson (2015), *Stonehenge: Making Sense of a Prehistoric Mystery*, p. 71 (Council for British Archaeology, York).

The timber structures that are so evident at the very first, Formative Stage of Stonehenge were put there just after the end of the earlier Neolithic period when the realms of the living and the dead were less clearly separated in people's minds. We know that prior to 3500 BC, sites like causewayed enclosures were visited by people who lived there for a few days or weeks on special occasions. These sites have provided evidence for food preparation, for feasting and also for burial and cremation. It was a period when people sought to integrate the spiritual lives of the dead with those of the living. The presence of the spirits of the ancestors provided stability and may also have helped to resolve disputes among the living. Indeed, we see further echoes of this integration of life and the afterlife in the frequent removal of bones from chambered tombs – taking them out into the community where they could be seen, and witnessed, in com-memoration ceremonies. It was believed that in this way the ancestors could keep a firm eye on the deeds of the living.

What one might think of as these old ways were quite rapidly replaced sometime shortly before 3000 BC by a new way of looking at life and death. In this new vision the two are now clearly separated into their own realms, symbolized as Ramilisonina has suggested, by wood and stone. This change was important because although it gave the ancestors an important role, it also conceded greater freedom to the living. Henceforward the stern traditions represented by ancestral practices would not intrude upon all aspects of daily life. People had acquired greater freedom to develop their own lives and societies. By the end of the period, around 1500 BC, they would be ready for a further step-change to even greater autonomy for the living. It was almost certainly no coincidence that this last innovation was accompanied by far more local control.

Now, if Ramilisonina and Parker Pearson's idea was correct – if, that is, the massive stones of Stonehenge symbolized the dead – there had to have been a timber counterpart to represent the living. And the obvious candidate has to be Woodhenge, a site just 2 miles (3.2 km) northeast of Stonehenge,

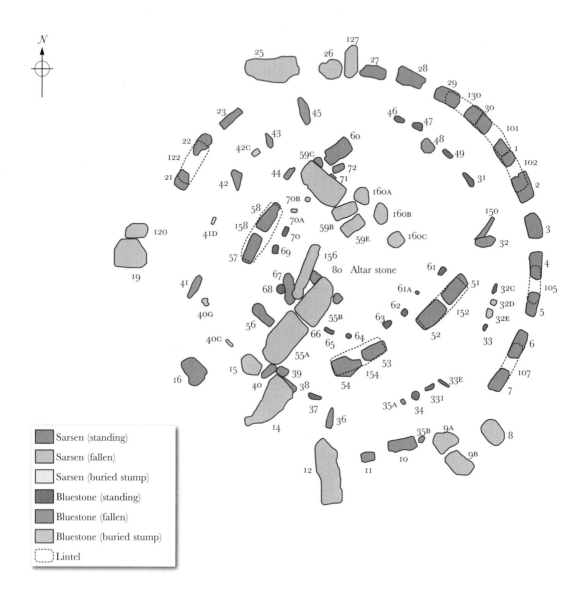

N

25　26　127　27　28　29　130　30　101　I　102　2
23　45　46　47　48　49　31　3
22　43　42C　60　59C　72　71　160A　160B　160C　32　150　4
122　21　44　42　59B　59E　158　70B　70A　70　69　156　80 Altar stone　61　61A　51　32C　105
120　41D　58　57　67　68　61A　62　63　52　152　32D　32E　33　5
19　41I　40G　56　55B　64　65　53　154　33E　6
40C　15　66　55A　39　38　37　36　35A　34　33I　107　7
16　40　14　12　11　10　35B　9A　9B　8

Sarsen (standing)
Sarsen (fallen)
Sarsen (buried stump)
Bluestone (standing)
Bluestone (fallen)
Bluestone (buried stump)
Lintel

Stonehenge with stone numbers

0   5   10 m

just outside Amesbury. Woodhenge, as it was soon to be called, was first recognized from aerial photos in 1925. It was excavated by Maud Cunnington between 1926 and 1929.[73] Then in 1966 it was proposed to reroute a stretch of the A345, from Amesbury to Marlborough, through the protected ancient henge of Durrington Walls, which lies immediately north of Woodhenge. This caused quite an uproar at the time, as Durrington Walls was known to be Britain's largest henge site. Eventually it was decided to completely excavate the route of the new road through the protected site, known as a Scheduled Ancient Monument. This work was directed by Geoffrey Wainwright as part of his hugely influential research into the henges of southwestern Britain.[74]

Wainwright's excavations revealed the presence of two massive and very complex multiple rings of timbers within the ditch and bank of the great henge. These were named the Northern and the Southern Circles. Taken at face value, then, Woodhenge and the two post circles at Durrington Walls provided the timber or living element of the timber-vs-stone theory. But somehow the two elements had to be linked. The idea was fine in theory, but how did it actually work out in the landscape? It was then that Parker Pearson had the idea that ultimately lead to the Stonehenge Riverside Project. He suggested that the timber structures of Woodhenge and Durrington Walls were linked to Stonehenge by a mystical or ceremonial route through the landscape. It began at Durrington Walls and then went down to a sinuous stretch of the River Avon which it followed downstream as far as the Stonehenge Avenue. It was by no means a direct route, but that was never its intention. Ultimately the final journey of the dead is always treated with solemnity, which is why modern hearses are expected to travel so slowly. From Stonehenge the dead would then be taken to their final resting place probably in a barrow out in the Stonehenge landscape. And as we will see shortly, it was Bluestonehenge that stood at the edge of the realm of the dead, down there on the riverbank. The River Avon was probably perceived as neither one thing nor the other, a dangerous place of transition, similar to the River Styx of classical myth, or Purgatory (neither Heaven nor Hell), of Roman Catholic Christianity.

The idea that the River Avon formed the link between death (the Avenue/Stonehenge) and the realm of the living, as represented by Durrington Walls and Woodhenge, would need to be confirmed, if not actually proved. It was unlikely that much would actually be discovered in the river itself, as its banks were constantly being built up and worn down by water. But maybe links could be found between the river and Durrington Walls, at one end, and the Avenue at the other. Between these two points the River Avon flowed, but in a very sinuous, meandering, and sometimes quite shallow, course. It was *so* indirect and circuitous that with hindsight it could have been designed to perform a mystical role. Such journeys were never meant to be easy. Indeed, when one of the archaeologists of the Riverside Project paddled his canoe along the route, with three passengers and a dog, it took him four hours to complete the journey.[75] And of course the modern River Avon is far more controlled than it would have been in prehistory.

I shall discuss the third element of the final ceremonial pilgrimage into the realm of the dead, the route from the river and then up the Avenue to Stonehenge and beyond, in the next chapter. Later in this chapter we will focus on the first part of that journey, within the realm of the living, as represented by Woodhenge and, more particularly, by Durrington Walls. But before we do that, we must return to the Stones, where some major changes are about to happen.

The years around 2500 BC were of immense significance in the Stonehenge story. To prehistorians the date also marks the end of the Neolithic and the start of the British Copper Age, or Chalcolithic. By this date the long tradition of using the area within the ditch as a cremation cemetery was drawing to a close. Had it been an ordinary site, one might have expected a gentle decline at this point, followed a few centuries later by

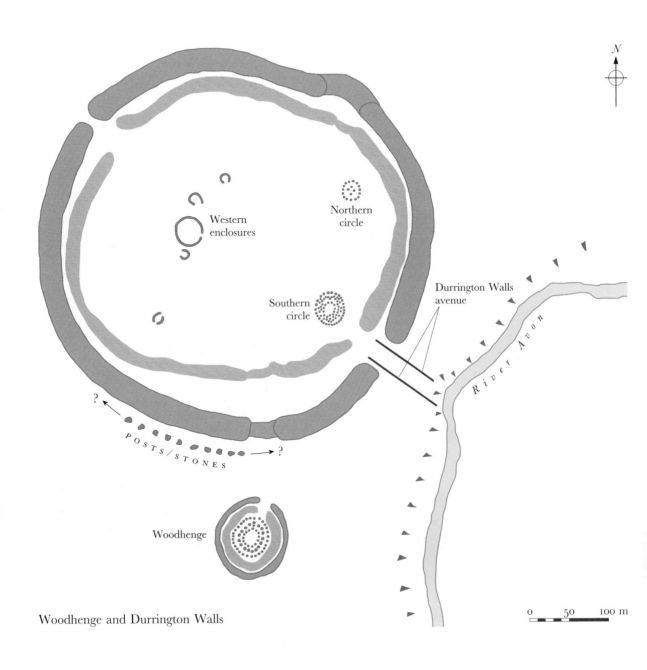

N

Western
enclosures

Northern
circle

Southern
circle

Durrington Walls
avenue

River Avon

? ←

P O S T S / S T O N E S

→ ?

Woodhenge

Woodhenge and Durrington Walls

0   50   100 m

THE GREAT STONES ARRIVE

abandonment. But it was not to be. Instead, there was a sudden explosion of activity, which almost certainly lasted less than a century and must have involved, quite literally, thousands of people.

The new Stonehenge that was created in Stage 2 is best illustrated by a plan. The basic layout is quite simple and the two main elements, the Sarsen Trilithon Horseshoe and the Sarsen Circle, remained substantially unaltered throughout Stages 2 to 5. From the outside it is difficult for the visitor to distinguish between the two – but this was probably semi-deliberate, inasmuch as those outside the central great Stones were not expected to see what was taking place within them. The principle is that of the Holy of Holies, or the altar rail, where only a select initiated few are allowed into the most hallowed area. The Trilithons are a U-shaped group of large three-stone sarsen settings (two uprights capped by a lintel) with the open top of the 'U' facing northeast towards the main entranceway (and later the Avenue). The sides of the U are formed by four separate three-stone settings. The base of the U, which forms the focus of the entire site, is the Great Trilithon. Today the only part of the Great Trilithon still in place is one of the two uprights, which stands appreciably taller than every other stone at Stonehenge. It has a stubby, neck-like protrusion, which is a tenon, which would have fitted into a matching mortice hole in the missing lintel. This is probably copied from a simple joint, which we know was employed in Neolithic carpentry. All the lintels were secured to their uprights in this way.

The slightly larger uprights of the five three-stone Trilithon settings in the horseshoe each supported just one lintel, which was located on a single tenon. This arrangement differed slightly from the way the lintels of the Sarsen Circle were attached. In this case the intention was to construct a continuous ring-beam of stone, so the ends of the individual lintels were shaped to butt up snugly to their neighbours. In addition each Sarsen Circle upright was proportionately slightly wider than those of the Trilithon settings and had two tenons to secure the abutting lintels. In the past many of the

Durrington Walls, located in the Stonehenge World Heritage Site.

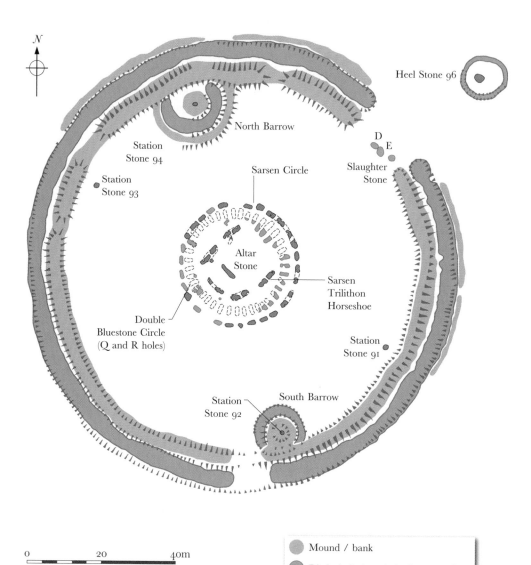

Heel Stone 96

North Barrow

Station
Stone 94

Station
Stone 93

Sarsen Circle

D
E

Slaughter
Stone

Altar
Stone

Sarsen
Trilithon
Horseshoe

Double
Bluestone Circle
(Q and R holes)

Station
Stone 91

Station
Stone 92

South Barrow

| 0 | 20 | 40m |

Stonehenge, Stage 2 *c.*2500 BC

Mound / bank

Ditch / pit / posthole / stone socket

Standing stone

stones of Stonehenge were broken up and taken away to be used in buildings elsewhere, so we cannot be absolutely certain that the Sarsen Circle was ever complete, although this does seem likely. Having said that, we saw in the previous chapter that at least one upright (Stone 11) appears to have been too small and short to have supported a sarsen lintel.

In 2011 the surfaces of all the stones at Stonehenge were laser-scanned in high definition to provide a detailed record of their shaping and subsequent damage.[76] Apart from its academic value, this survey allows future conservators to assess the extent to which the site is being affected by environmental factors, such as acid rain and lichen growth. Although there has been much speculation over the years about how the Stones were fashioned, this report was able to isolate no fewer than thirteen different techniques, or patterns of wear, that ranged from splitting entire stones (there were three examples of this) to coarse dressing, flaking, then grinding and even polishing. With the exception of the grinding and polishing, which is only found on the lowest 2 metres (six ft), most of the shaping and dressing appears to have been done before the Stones were erected. The coarse dressing, which produced rippled grooves separated by low ridges, can be seen quite readily by visitors to the monument, especially on some of the fallen stones and on the sides and inner faces of the larger uprights.

The dressing of the bluestones is very different from that of the sarsens, with a far more limited repertoire of just three identifiable techniques, all of which involved picking or hammering. Unlike sarsen, bluestone (usually Preseli Spotted Dolerite, a chemically altered volcanic rock) splits naturally into block-shaped pieces, and so does not require heavy-duty shaping.

The laser survey has also given us some exciting new insights into the way that the Stones were meant to be viewed and appreciated. It has long been known, for example, that the Great Trilithon, at the base of the Horseshoe of Trilithons, was notably taller than the other three surviving settings, but the new survey clearly demonstrated that the two Trilithons

[opposite above]
A general view of the
Stones from the south
showing how the density of
their concentration would
have made viewing the
interior very difficult.

[opposite below]
This view from the south
shows the contrast in size
between the single upright
of the Great Trilithon
(centre) and two Trilithon
settings of the Horseshoe
(on either side). Note the
smaller size of the two
uprights to the left of the
picture, which formed part
of the Sarsen Circle. Note
too the very small bluestone
upright immediately to the
left of the Great Trilithon
upright.

nearest the entranceway were shorter than the two alongside the Great
Trilithon. So there was a gradual increase in height from northeast to
southwest. This arrangement contrasts with the horizontal lintel of the
Sarsen Circle and draws the eye towards the Great Trilithon, which was
arranged to frame the midwinter solstice sunset. As we will see shortly, Stonehenge was never just about the midsummer sunrise.

The subtlety of the stone-dressing revealed by the laser scan was
remarkable. It was apparent, for example, that the stones of the Trilithon
Horseshoe were dressed in ways that enhanced their architectural unity and
drew attention to their alignment on the solstice.[77] Often the stones had been
carefully matched for size, working and colour. A detailed examination of the
stone-working techniques hinted at the possibility that the Trilithons might
not have been prepared by the same groups that worked on the Sarsen
Circle. This might indicate a gap between the construction of the two;
having said that, however, they do form such a coherent, integrated structure
that this seems unlikely (to this author, at least). It could also be argued that as
the Trilithons lay at the heart of Stonehenge, the people who erected them
might have been of higher status, or were senior in the tribal religious
hierarchy to the rest of the workforce. Or even more subtle factors could
have been at play.

At Seahenge, for example, the central inverted oak tree was worked by
different axes from those used to shape the timbers of the circular wall that
surrounded it. Then tree-ring studies demonstrated that a few of the timbers
forming the encircling wall had been cut from the central oak when it was
being prepared for insertion in the ground. When they were examined
Maisie Taylor discovered that these timbers had been worked with the same
axes as the central oak.[78] This would suggest that it was the tree that was
considered special, and not its position in the structure. Maybe it was the
colour and quality of the stone used for the Trilithons that dictated who
should work them, rather than their eventual location at the centre of
Stonehenge.

Low sunlight reveals the rippled shallow grooves that resulted when the surface of this fallen sarsen was dressed by flaking-off large chips with a hard hammer-stone, a technique, known as coarse dressing. Sarsen can be worked far more readily when freshly removed from below the ground.

The thirty upright stones of the Sarsen Circle had been carefully selected to provide an absolutely level circular lintel, which took into account the gently sloping ground surface.[79] Today seventeen of the original uprights are still standing, whereas just six of the original thirty lintels are still in place.[80] The laser scanning revealed that the exterior surfaces were less carefully dressed than the interior, but efforts were made to remove the darker, grey weathered exterior, to reveal the paler, pinkish natural stone beneath. The finer finishing of the interior faces would have been necessary, as these were seen more closely than the outside faces, which could not have been scrutinized in any detail by people standing at some distance outside – most probably beyond the ditch and its external bank.

Considerable efforts were made to dress the sides of the vertical sarsens to give an impression, still visible today, of straight, parallel and well-set uprights.[81] But the Sarsen Circle was never a simple structure. Close examination of the way the uprights were trimmed suggests that the vertical stones and their lintels, at the points where the circle straddled the main northeast–southwest solsticial axis, had been carefully trimmed and straightened in order to enhance and frame the sun on the longest and shortest days. The approach to the Stones from the northeast, along that axis and down the Avenue, was made more impressive by the careful selection and dressing of the stones used to form the circle in its northeastern segments. These would have been the first seen by visitors and they are noticeably more regularly shaped and finely finished than their counterparts to the southwest. This would further emphasize that the midwinter sunset was meant to be viewed from within the Trilithon Horseshoe, where, as we have seen, the Great Trilithon had been carefully prepared to frame it.[82]

People have been speculating about Stonehenge, eclipses and solar alignments since William Stukeley in the early eighteenth century judged that Stonehenge was aligned in the direction of the midsummer sunrise.[83] But speculation gave way to more science-based observation and prediction with the appearance of early computers in the mid-1960s.[84] The best-known of these new studies was published in a book with a far from understated title, *Stonehenge Decoded*, by Gerald S. Hawkins.[85] Hawkins (and his collaborator John B. White) was able to make use of the then state-of-the-art Harvard-Smithsonian IBM computer and the book proved a massive success, with huge sales worldwide. Hawkins suggested that Stonehenge included numerous solar and lunar alignments, which may or may not have been relevant in prehistory. He also famously described the site as a 'Neolithic computer' – which it most certainly was not.[86] Soon it became clear that Stonehenge was by no means unique and that many other megalithic and timber-built sites had solar alignments. Initially the response to these discoveries was appropriate to an age where silicon-chip technology dominated the news: it was widely held that prehistoric people were astronomers who used their religious sites as observatories to predict solar events, such as eclipses. But with time came reason.

Today prehistorians are agreed that the solar and lunar orientations have more in common with astrology than with scientific astronomy. Yes, the stones are indeed set accurately in locations that must be based on observation and recording, but their purpose is not to study the movement of solar bodies, so much as to draw the inhabited world closer to the wider universe of nature. At this stage in prehistory, people would probably not have been aware that Britain was an island or that the world was a planet. The sun, moon and stars would have been considered as integral elements of the environment in which communities lived their daily lives; they would have been viewed as part of nature, rather like celestial mountain ranges. And like the cycle of the seasons, they helped to provide the framework for family life, for work – and for thought and imagination. It was a very rich way of looking at the world.

The northeast-to-southwest (midsummer sunrise and midwinter sunset) axis was Stonehenge's principal alignment – and of course it had ancient

THE GREAT STONES ARRIVE

beginnings. But as we saw in Chapter 4 there were also other astronomical alignments, although these were often approximate, rather than precise. These were given greater precision in Stage 2, with the appearance of the Station Stones (nos. 91–4), which were aligned on major moonrise and moonset events.[87] They were placed just inside the inner bank of the ditch and together they formed a rectangle. This arrangement was accurately aligned on the familiar midwinter sunset/midsummer sunrise. The southwest side pointed in the direction of the moon's most southerly rise and its most northerly setting. The significance of Station Stones 94 and 92 (the most northerly and southerly respectively) was enhanced by the construction of small semi-circular ditches, with mounds, today known as the North and South Barrows.

Other Stage 2 developments included the placing of three stones, including the so-called Slaughter Stone (a colourful Victorian name), across the main entranceway and the possible setting of the Heel Stone (once one of a pair) in its current position.[88] The two great sarsen structures aside, the other main event in Stage 2 was the erection of a double ring of bluestones ,which ran in the space between the Sarsen Circle and the inner Trilithon Horseshoe. The stones for this new setting were almost certainly removed from both the Aubrey Holes and Bluestonehenge. They were then set in the ground as a double ring, in stone-holes known as the Q and R Holes. This arrangement of stone-holes was first revealed by Professor Richard Atkinson in his excavations in 1954.[89]

By Stage 2 Stonehenge is very much a building, an example of coordinated prehistoric architecture, and in this it contrasts markedly with its more episodic beginnings in the Formative Stage. By 2500 BC large numbers of people were needed for its construction and they had to be accommodated and fed. Until the Stonehenge Riverside Project burst upon the scene, almost nothing was known about these people. In some respects they were like the navvies who built Britain's railways in the 1840s: they were unsung pioneers. But now we have discovered where they lived –

An aerial view showing the different Trilithon settings of the stones.

the Neolithic equivalents of the Victorian navvy camps.[90] But there is one crucial difference between the Victorian railway-builders and the Neolithic henge-makers. The navvies were hired labour and were paid for their back-breaking work. The builders of Stonehenge lived a far less oppressive existence. They were doing something they believed in, and we will learn that their lifestyle was more appropriate to a pilgrim than an underpaid workman.

We come now to what has to be the most important discovery in the history of Stonehenge research. It provides strong support, if not actual proof, for the symbolic journey from life (timber) to death (stone), but it also – and at long last – gives us a glimpse into the lives of the thousands of people who constructed this most remarkable prehistoric monument.

All good research is structured around an important question. Frequently it provides results that turn out to be the answers to slightly different questions. And that is what happened in this instance. After assembling a team of researchers that became the Stonehenge Riverside Project, Mike Parker Pearson wanted to ascertain if his Madagascan friend's idea about a journey from life to death could be tested in the field. The obvious place to start was the banks of the River Avon near the huge henge of Durrington Walls. The first season of research began with a survey, which was followed in 2004 by excavation. This provided abundant evidence for later Neolithic activity, in the form of flints, pottery and other finds but there was little by way of actual archaeological features, such as ditches, banks or stone-holes.[91] They would soon discover that this was because they had placed their trenches too close to the riverside, where water had caused much damage through erosion.

In 2005 they positioned their main trench further up the slope, away from the river and closer to the great banks of Durrington Walls. And here they came down on what they soon realized was an intact Neolithic house floor.[92] It was to prove a momentous discovery. Intact Neolithic house floors that have never been damaged by ploughing are exceedingly rare in southern

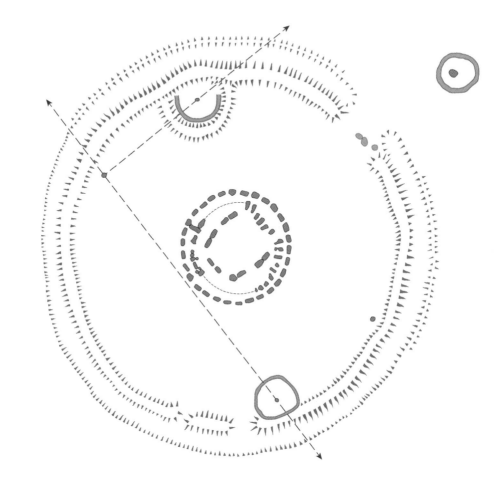

0   20   40m

Plan of Astronomical Alignments,
Stonehenge, Stage 2 *c.*2620–2480 BC

A group of four Neolithic houses from Durrington Walls, as reconstructed at the Stonehenge Visitor Centre.

Britain and here was one just outside Britain's largest henge. There could be no doubt: at some stage in its history, Durrington Walls had been more than a ceremonial site. Little did the diggers in that first trench of 2005 realize that their house would turn out to be part of an enormous, and very short-lived, settlement, which would prove to be precisely contemporary with the erection of the great stones at Stonehenge. By the end of the season, it was becoming increasingly apparent that these houses were where the Stonehenge workforce had lived. Two years later, in 2007, I made my first visit to the excavations and by then the extent of the Durrington village was becoming evident: it was by far the largest in Britain and one of the biggest in Europe.[93]

The Riverside Project's excavations showed that the houses built for (and by?) the Stonehenge Stage 2 workforce, or workforces, were not the often ramshackle, sometimes ex-army sheds used by the railway navvies of Victorian times. Instead, they lived in proper houses whose design can be closely paralleled across the British Isles.[94] The excavations of 2004–7 revealed nine square houses measuring about 5.3 metres (17 ft) across. The walls were made from posts set about 30 cm (or a foot) apart and interwoven with wattlework, which was then coated with a plaster-like daub, made from pounded chalk, soil and animal dung. Wide eaves would have been essential to keep this material dry. There were wooden box-beds around the walls. At the centre of each house was a rectangular hearth and, in at least one case, two depressions could be detected where people knelt while tending to a fire. The houses were not standardized nor uniform, and some were clearly of higher status than others. Excellent reconstructions have been built outside the new Stonehenge Visitor Centre.

Most prehistoric settlements in Britain are often quite long-lived. The Iron Age village I excavated in Peterborough, at Fengate, in the 1970s, featured houses that were positioned on top of ones that had been abandoned; rubbish pits intercut them and new paths were driven through collapsed buildings.[95] But, unusually, the Durrington Walls settlement

THE GREAT STONES ARRIVE

Interior of a reconstructed Neolithic house from Durrington Walls showing the central hearth, the framework for a wooden bed, which would have been covered with a stuffed woven or fleece mattress. Note the shelves at the back wall opposite the entrance. In many Neolithic houses in Orkney these shelves would have served as family shrines or altars, where special objects were displayed.

showed none of these tell-tale signs. All the houses seemed to respect the presence of the other buildings around them. Indeed, it was soon clear that all had been standing at the same time. Another indication that the settlement was short-lived was provided by those pits that were dug outside each house to provide chalk for making and repairing both the walls and ,possibly more importantly, the floors. In one instance, microscopic examination of the chalk floor showed that it had been built up in seven distinct episodes – presumably these were laid every time the building was reoccupied, which other evidence suggests was for a limited period of weeks or at most months, in the autumn and spring (the quiet periods in the farming calendar). The evidence from the floors fits well with what was found when the houses' chalk pits were excavated. These were enlarged out of the previous year's pit and the largest group consisted of some twelve pits – which might suggest that the village was occupied for at most one or two decades. This short lifespan was supported by radiocarbon dates, which showed the settlement was in existence between 2480 and 2460 BC.[96]

Further excavation and geophysical survey suggests that the Durrington settlement probably held about 1,000 houses, giving a population of at least 4,000 people. Recent analyses of the food bones and the residues found adhering to pottery suggest that the workforce at Durrington ate very well indeed.[97] Pork was popular and many of the pigs had been slaughtered in the autumn or winter. This fits well with the alignment of two timber henge-like circles whose entrances faced along the axis of the mid-winter sunrise. All the evidence suggests that the Herculean task of erecting the great stones at Stonehenge took place in the late autumn and winter, and probably over a ten-year period. By any standards it was a remarkably efficient project, which was carried out by people who shared a very strong sense of purpose. We will get a better understanding of the strength of the ideas that motivated them when we start to contemplate the final journey from life to death. Even though we can only glimpse fleeting reflections of their former beliefs, they still possess an extraordinary power over the imagination. Over 4,000 years later, it is not difficult to appreciate why so many people found them irresistible.

[overleaf]
The Wiltshire Champion Coursing Meeting at Stonehenge by G. B. Godard. *The Illustrated London News*, 11 November 1865.

6

THE JOURNEY FROM LIFE TO DEATH:
STAGE 3
[FROM 2400 BC]

Even though the village for the workforce at Stonehenge was relatively short-lived, Durrington Walls continued to be a major centre where people assembled to accompany their loved ones on their last journey. Despite the use of stone at Stonehenge, Durrington Walls (with Woodhenge, directly opposite its southern entrance) continued to be constructed from timber. This must surely be significant and confirms the timber = life, stone = death hypothesis. The orientations of the various timber circles share solsticial alignments that echo those at Stonehenge, although the focus is towards the midwinter sunrise rather than the midsummer sunrise. This might symbolize the rising of the sun at the end of life and the start of the journey towards a new life.

The recent discovery of a slightly curved row of stone- or large post-holes, buried immediately outside the southern circuit of the Durrington Walls henge bank, is a striking new feature, which might represent a circle of posts that preceded the later ditch and bank.[98] One of the Riverside Project's biggest discoveries, the much shorter Durrington Walls Avenue, would have guided processions down the slope from the eastern exit from the Durrington settlement (and the later henge) to the River Avon, for the first part of the journey from life to death. Just like the Stonehenge Avenue, which follows a group of deep grooves in the subsoil, the new Durrington Avenue follows a naturally deposited gravel surface, which, in turn, is lined up on the midsummer sunset – which is entirely appropriate to the start of a journey at the end of life. This avenue was clearly meant to have given the departing soul a good send-off. It was 15 metres (50 ft) wide and flanked by banks on both sides. It was clearly a major processional way and intended to accommodate large crowds of mourners, who would not have been able to accompany the body for the next and most difficult part of the journey, along the turbulent River Avon.

As the crow flies, the distance from Durrington Walls to the point where the Stonehenge Avenue joins the River Avon at Bluestonehenge is just 1½ miles (2.5 km), but the river takes a much more circuitous route – more than doubling that distance. We saw in Chapter 5 that Bluestonehenge was constructed in Stage 1 around 2950 BC. In its first phase, Bluestonehenge consisted of a circle of about twenty-five bluestones that had been transported to the site on the river's edge, fully dressed and shaped. No dressing or chipping debris was found in and around the stone-holes. At this point in Stonehenge's history of development the Bluestonehenge circle would have stood on its own, as the Avenue had yet to be constructed. The posts and bluestone circle at Stonehenge would have been just out of sight, about 1 mile (2.2 km) to the northwest. The Bluestonehenge stones were packed into their holes using variable techniques and packing material, which suggests that in Stage 1 the work may have been done by individual communities, rather than the more centralized workforce that undertook the heavy building tasks of Stage 2.[99]

The stones at Bluestonehenge were removed around 2400 BC and were most probably taken to Stonehenge, where it seems they were used to make a new inner bluestone circle, of twenty-five stones. If all the bluestones used in the various settings at Stonehenge at different periods are counted, the maximum number comes out at about eighty. Given the huge distance these stones had to be transported, it seems highly probable that these were the stones brought in for the Aubrey Holes and Bluestonehenge, back in Stage 1. Once the stones had been removed from Bluestonehenge a new henge was created on the site, consisting of a ditch with an external bank and an entranceway that faced northeast, just like at Stonehenge. This new henge is known as the West Amesbury henge and it was positioned centrally, at the end of the newly constructed Stonehenge Avenue, which was constructed shortly after 2400 BC. It is still a major feature in the landscape, especially when seen from the air: two parallel ditches with banks alongside their inner (and probably) outer edges and a central roadway almost 20 metres wide – closely comparable with the Durrington Avenue, although the Stonehenge Avenue was very much longer (1¾ miles or 2.8 km).

An aerial of the
excavation at West
Amesbury Henge /
Bluestonehenge.

The manner in which the bluestones were erected in the new inner circle at Stonehenge, by individual working parties, provides a hint that they may have played a different role from the much larger sarsen structures around them. The sarsens were static, the bluestones mobile. But there were deeper symbolisms – one can gain an impression of this if one is lucky enough to be able to walk through the centre of Stonehenge alone. Indeed, I had a similar experience when I came on set one evening while we were filming the documentary *Foamhenge*, but in this instance the feeling was heightened by the different colours of the Styrofoam 'bluestones' and 'sarsens'. I do not think it is putting it too strongly, but I could not help feeling that the smaller bluestones were in some way a human-scale 'presence' – and certainly when compared with the towering sarsens around them. I am not suggesting for one moment that the bluestones were somehow alive spiritually, but their human-sized scale, especially when contrasted with the sarsen Trilithons, seemed – how can I put it? – a welcoming presence. I can imagine how an awe-struck prehistoric pilgrim might have found reassurance and comfort when standing beside one of them.

I know for a fact that other prehistorians have shared the feeling that the bluestones were put there to provide some sort of human-scale presence against the massive sarsen representation of time, the landscape, the sun and moon, seems to loom over and enshroud anyone standing in the centre of Stonehenge. Maybe the human-sized bluestones did represent actual people? If so, they would probably have been prominent ancestors: the kind of men and women whose bones, in earlier Neolithic times, would have been removed from chambered tombs and taken out into the community. If this idea has any validity, it might help explain why the bluestones were moved so frequently – because it was the individual represented by the stone that mattered. A modern equivalent might be a statue in a town, which would be moved if, for example, a road was enlarged. In medieval and early post-medieval times, memorials in churches were frequently shifted to make way for grander new additions.

A further question arises from the suggestion that the bluestones might have represented actual individuals. Did people come from the Preseli Mountains with their bluestones, to create Stonehenge, or did communities from Salisbury Plain, who would have known about the fissures in the rock beneath the Avenue, and other local myths and legends, journey north to collect them? If we make the simple assumption that rocks = people, then we must also accept that a large proportion of the Lake District Neolithic population travelled east from the Langdale quarries, bearing their distinctive greenstone axes. And that seems most unlikely. I would suggest that the bluestones were considered holy, because of links to the realm of the ancestors provided by their remote, liminal quarries, and that they acquired their new individual identities when they were erected in the Aubrey Holes and at Bluestonehenge, shortly after 3000 BC. These identities might well have changed when the eighty bluestones were moved and re-erected (often more than once) in the centre of Stonehenge, half a millennium later.

The construction of the inner circle of bluestones and the Avenue were the biggest structural modifications to Stonehenge during Stage 3. Elsewhere, Bluestonehenge and Woodhenge were surrounded by big ditches and banks, which can be seen as a way of somehow sealing them off, yet memorializing them at the same time. These developments took place at a time when British prehistory was going through some major changes. It is tempting to suggest that the stability evident at Stonehenge reflected its role in society at large, where it would have stood as a prominent symbol of enduring traditions and social cohesion.

Stage 3 begins around 2400 BC. We have now left the age of stone and are in the first age of metal: the Copper Age. The Copper Age was relatively short-lived in Britain: maybe three or so centuries after 2500 BC. From 2200 BC it gave way to the Early Bronze Age, which in turn came to an end around 1500 BC – a date which saw the rapid decline of both henges and the tradition of ritual landscapes. The arrival of metal-working would have its impact over time, especially as regards carpentry and wood-working, where the new copper and bronze axes were a notable improvement on the easily chipped and shattered flint and stone axes of the Neolithic.

Weaponry, on the other hand, was only slightly improved. The new metal daggers were slightly sharper than their flint predecessors, but stone arrowheads continued in use well into the Bronze Age. The main improvement was one of appearance: brightly gleaming, freshly cast copper and bronze daggers must have looked so spectacular to people who had grown used to grey and pale brown flint. Perhaps the biggest impact of the new metal-working technology, around 2500 BC, would have been the improvements it brought to the control of heat and very high temperatures, which came with the introduction of small furnaces and bellows. Copper, the principal (90 per cent) ingredient of bronze, an alloy with 10 per cent tin, melts at 1981° Fahrenheit (1083° Celsius). This greater control of very high temperatures soon led to new styles of much better-quality, thin-walled pottery, of which the best-known types are the lavishly decorated drinking cups, known as Bell Beakers (after their distinctively flared profile).

Bell Beakers were part of the culture of the first people to introduce the arts of metal-working to Britain. They brought their new techniques and ideas with them from mainland Europe. Most human cultures bury their dead in distinctive ways; indeed, these are important components of a community's identity – and the people of the Bell Beaker culture were no exception. Their new rites involved a switch away from cremation to inhumation beneath a round barrow in a single grave. Men and women of higher status would be accompanied by rich grave goods, which almost always included one or more Beaker vessels, plus flint or metal daggers and copper or bronze axes. Archery was an essential feature of life at the time and very finely flaked flint arrowheads are often included as grave goods, along with beautifully polished stone archers' wrist guards, sometimes embellished with gold studs. There is

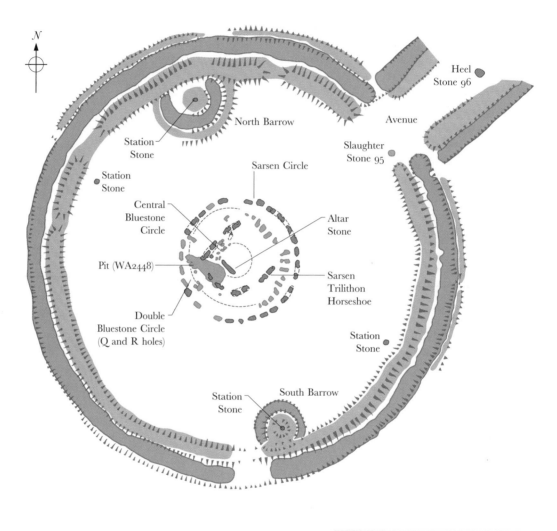

N

Heel
Stone 96

North Barrow

Avenue

Station
Stone

Station
Stone

Sarsen Circle

Slaughter
Stone 95

Central
Bluestone
Circle

Altar
Stone

Pit (WA2448)

Sarsen
Trilithon
Horseshoe

Double
Bluestone Circle
(Q and R holes)

Station
Stone

Station
Stone

South Barrow

0   20   40m

Stonehenge, Stage 3 *c.*2400 BC

Mound / bank

Ditch / pit / posthole / stone socket

Standing stone

still some doubt as to the initial status of Beaker-using people within British society, but in the centuries after about 2500 BC many of the items that appear in early Beaker graves are found widely distributed in graves and in settlements across Britain. This would suggest that what might have begun as an exclusive elite soon became integrated within wider Bronze Age society.

A remarkable Beaker-period burial was found in the Stonehenge ditch, about ten metres back from the northern terminal, at the main entranceway, during excavations in 1978.[100] Most single-grave inhumations of the second half of the third millennium BC are of people who have died without violence, but this was a rare exception. The body was that of a man who had been buried in the usual manner of the time, with his legs bent and one arm across his chest. As Beaker-period bodies go, his corpse had not been very carefully arranged in the grave, which had been dug about halfway into the ditch filling. Unusually he was not accompanied by a Beaker pot, but we can be certain of the date because of three distinctively shaped (so-called barbed-and-tanged) arrowheads, which had entered his chest from three different sides of his body. This might suggest he was shot by three separate people, as one archer would be unlikely to reload that quickly. We can also be quite certain that the arrows struck his body while the bone was still living, because the tip of one was still present in the fourth left rib. The bone is still lifted and buckled – giving it a horribly recent appearance.[101] All three arrows are missing their tips.

But the item that was most informative was found lying alongside and parallel with his left wrist. It was a polished stone wrist-guard – an essential part of an archer's equipment, which protects the inside of the arm that is holding the bow from being repeatedly slapped by the bow-string. The body has given radiocarbon dates of 2400–2140 BC. It is hard not to see this burial as a symbol of ownership or possession of some sort. His grave was placed close by the main entranceway – bodies are quite often found in ditches near gateways in Bronze Age field systems and they are thought to symbolize that a particular group owned, or farmed, a given parcel of land.[102] If it was not the dead archer himself, then more likely it was his killers who controlled access to Stonehenge.

Issues relating to the control of monuments, land and ultimately people were gaining in importance from the middle of the third millennium BC, not just at Stonehenge, but right across prehistoric Europe. However, it was not just about the rise of powerful individuals – warlords or 'Big Men' – as some have supposed. It was a period when pre-existing tribal communities were becoming more ranked and hierarchical, as the population of Britain steadily increased. The arrival of the new technologies surrounding metalworking, controlled by the people who used Beaker pottery, undoubtedly accelerated this process of regional centralization and consolidation further. Smaller communities were being absorbed into larger groupings to form regional tribal confederations. In most instances these new arrangements would have provided greater stability and larger workforces to carry out major projects, such as the building of Stonehenge. But when conflicts did arise, they would probably have been worse, because the opposed communities were growing more cohesive and self-confident.

A fascinating insight into the sort of people who were now becoming increasingly important to the Stonehenge story has recently been revealed by the discovery of yet another male burial with arrows. This time, however, they had not been shot into him. In May 2002 the body of a man aged between thirty-five and fifty was found some 3 miles (5 km) south of Stonehenge, just outside Amesbury. The Amesbury Archer, as he soon became known, was buried with many high-status objects, including fifteen top-quality flint arrowheads, two polished stone wrist-guards and no less than five complete Beaker vessels.[103] The burial has been radiocarbon dated to 2470–2280 BC (almost precisely contemporary with the burial in the Stonehenge ditch). Two beautiful basket-shaped gold earrings had been placed in the grave at his knees. One might have expected a man of this

importance to have been surrounded by grave goods, which, having been made especially for the occasion, proclaimed his status however, three of the Beaker pots showed clear signs of having been used, most probably in ordinary domestic life.[104]

A further sign that the Amesbury Archer had been a member of a family, and had lived within a community, was revealed when the body of another young man, aged twenty-five to thirty, who had been buried in a separate but accompanying grave, was closely examined. One might have supposed that he had been a slave who had been sacrificed to serve his master in the afterlife. But although his grave held far fewer grave goods, it did include two gold earrings, similar to those worn by the older man and also placed at his knees. They must surely have been symbols, not just of rank, but of family too.

The nature of their actual relationship was only revealed when the two skeletons were examined forensically.[105] This study showed that the foot bones of both skeletons were affected by a medical condition known as 'bilateral non-osseous calcaneo-navicular coalition'. This rare condition is passed on within immediate families and over several generations. This might suggest that the Amesbury Archer was accompanied in the afterlife by his son, or perhaps by a younger brother.

We shall close this chapter with a fascinating glimpse into the lives and backgrounds of these closely related men. Human teeth do most of their growing in childhood and the composition of their enamel will reflect the water a child drinks. Analyses of their tooth enamels suggested that the older man was brought up in southeast or west Germany. By way of contrast, his younger relative had been raised in southern England (his teeth showed he had drunk water from chalklands).[106] This discovery is important, because it tells us that the new networks of power and control that started to appear after 2500 BC did not spring up out of nowhere. We know from other evidence that travel was growing in popularity at the outset of the Bronze Age, and it should come as no surprise that the new Beaker presence may well have included people from continental Europe. It was the beginning of a process that would continue for over 4,000 years. It is now well established that elite British families in Bronze Age, Iron Age and Roman times benefited from social and economic contacts – which frequently included marriages – with their counterparts in mainland Europe. Doubtless such long-distance marriages were seen as being exotic, perhaps even mystical, too.[107]

But it would be a mistake to view the emerging new elites through modern eyes. These were not entrepreneurs or high-profile sportsmen. They were people who came from traditional tribal backgrounds and would have been constrained by family, marriage and other ties. Their success would doubtless have reflected some glory on themselves, but the main credit would have gone to the clan or tribe they belonged to. Stonehenge had always represented people, but within their social setting. Even in its final stages it continued to be more about stability and cohesion than mere physical control, or indeed celebrity.

[overleaf]
An inward view of Stonehenge 'from behind the High Altar', 1760.

7

LATER DEVELOPMENT: STAGES 4 AND 5

[2100–1500 BC]

The date is 2100 BC and we are now a century into the Bronze Age. The evidence suggests that Stonehenge not only continued to be used much later than most other henges, but somehow it still retained much of its earlier popularity, power and influence, to judge from the great wealth evident in the barrows that surround it. The use of the landscape away from Salisbury Plain had been undergoing major changes from about 2000 BC, when the first large-scale field systems came into being in places like the Thames Valley and the lowlands of eastern England. By 1500 BC this major intensification of agriculture was making itself felt locally. Eventually the barrows surrounding Stonehenge were to give way to the irresistible advance of agriculture, which was increasingly required to feed a steadily growing population. We will discuss these developments more fully in the next chapter.

The Stonehenge ritual landscape had now become the largest cemetery of burial mounds (barrows) in Britain. By this period the single-grave, men-only barrows, which were so characteristic of the Copper Age and earlier Beaker-using families, were being replaced by larger barrows, which often contained the remains of women and children, too.

The layout of the stones within Stonehenge itself continued to be very conservative. The Sarsen Circle and the Trilithon Horseshoe, laid out four centuries previously, remained in use largely unaltered, but a new circle of bluestones was laid out, which followed the inner edge of the Sarsen Circle more closely. Also during Stage 4 (2100–1600 BC) another setting of blue-stones, this time in an oval, was erected inside the Trilithon Horseshoe. Somewhat later in Stage 4 the bluestones at the northeastern end of the oval were removed, to leave a U-shaped setting that echoed the much larger Trilithon Horseshoe immediately outside and above it. The open side of this U-shaped setting faced towards the main entranceway and the midsummer sunrise.

Outside the area of the Stones, lengths of the Avenue ditches, especially down the slope towards the River Avon, were recut during this period, but this does not seem to have been a major emptying-out of the entire ditch.[108] One suspects that the intention was to 'freshen up' the pale (and in places natural), chalky banks, which defined the edges of the processional way, wherever they had become obscured by turf growth. These works, however minor, do show us that the Avenue and the processional route from Durrington Walls and Woodhenge continued to be an essential part of what one might call the Stonehenge experience.

The final phase of modification at Stonehenge took place in Stage 5 (1600–1500 BC). Apart from the creation of the two new bluestone settings (the ring and the inner oval) early in Stage 4, very little else seems to have been changed for almost five centuries. But shortly after 1600 BC two circles of pits, known as the Y and Z Holes, were dug in the open space between the Sarsen Circle and the ditch's inner bank.

The Y and Z Holes are, frankly, a mystery. They do not appear ever to have held bluestones nor wooden posts. In fact, they were dug and then simply abandoned and allowed to fill in by natural means. The fine sediment they contained probably blew in from the new fields that were now being ploughed around them. When excavated by Hawley in the 1920s, some of the Y and Z Holes were found to contain antler picks, a proportion of which, radiocarbon dates have shown, were already antiques.[109] Another unusual feature was the discovery, at the bottom of many holes, of fragments of bluestone (and of sarsen), which Professor Atkinson in the 1950s believed had been placed there, probably as offerings.[110] Today most prehistorians would, perhaps reluctantly, agree with Atkinson's suggestion that the Y and Z Holes had been dug to receive yet another setting of bluestones – but that this simply failed to happen. This must surely indicate that the social organization and the practical infrastructure that had gradually developed to service this most remarkable of prehistoric monuments was now, and quite rapidly, starting to disintegrate.

It would probably be a big mistake to think that the seeming stability of the main monument meant that Stonehenge and the ritual landscape

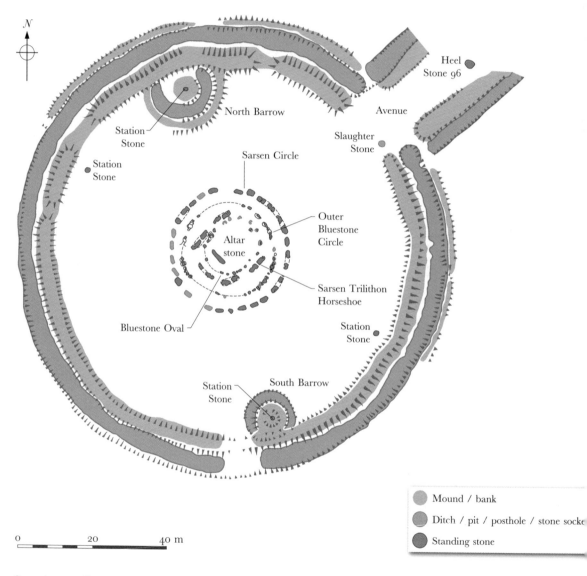

N

Heel
Stone 96

North Barrow

Station
Stone

Avenue

Station
Stone

Slaughter
Stone

Sarsen Circle

Outer
Bluestone
Circle

Altar
stone

Sarsen Trilithon
Horseshoe

Bluestone Oval

Station
Stone

Station
Stone

South Barrow

0   20   40 m

Mound / bank

Ditch / pit / posthole / stone socket

Standing stone

Stonehenge, Stage 4 *c.*2100 BC

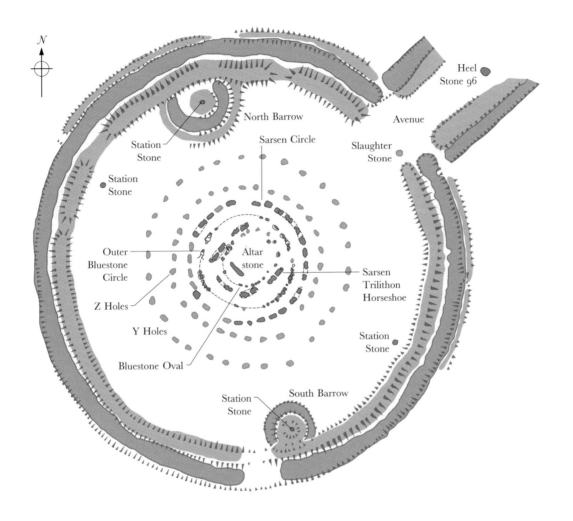

N

Heel
Stone 96

North Barrow

Sarsen Circle

Avenue

Station
Stone

Slaughter
Stone

Station
Stone

Outer
Bluestone
Circle

Altar
stone

Sarsen
Trilithon
Horseshoe

Z Holes

Y Holes

Station
Stone

Bluestone Oval

Station
Stone

South Barrow

0   20   40 m

Stonehenge, Stage 5 *c.*1600 BC

A few of the Normanton
Down group of burial
mounds (barrows), as seen
from Stonehenge. In this
image four of the mounds
have been caught by
sunlight and are clearly
visible in the middle
distance. Even without the
sunlight, they can readily be
seen from the Stones.

surrounding it was not being used. If anything one could suggest the opposite: that the slow-down in alterations to the main site was a consequence of its very popularity as a means of transferring the souls of the dead from the world of the living to the realm of the ancestors. So instead of tweaking the arrangement of the Stones, people were now putting their energies into the ceremonies themselves and, of course, into the graves within the hundreds of new burial mounds (barrows) that were being raised in the landscape around the Stones. There are about 350 Bronze Age barrows in just the protected area of the Stonehenge World Heritage Site.[111] So let us now take a quick look at what was happening in one particular area of this landscape.

We saw in Chapter 3 that the Normanton Down group of barrows, which can still be seen from the Stones in a clear row in the middle distance, was connected to Stonehenge by way of the southerly continuation of the solsticial alignment. This alignment followed a low brow-like ridge, which swings south and east to join Normanton Down, one of the low hills that surrounds the Stonehenge basin. Some of these round barrows were excavated 200 years ago by the pioneering archaeologists William Cunnington and Sir Richard Colt Hoare, and they have been the subject of an intriguing recent study.[112] The informal but closely packed line of over twenty barrows included four that contained exceptionally rich grave goods. These were placed alongside male bodies that had been arranged in the ground, in a crouched position, with knees drawn up and arms placed across the chest. Each body was accompanied by high-quality metal objects, which included bronze or copper daggers, knives and axes. Many had ornamented hilts, and although fabric and leather did not survive in the soil, the fastenings for belts and tunics, plus toggles, beads and other ornaments, suggest that the bodies had been laid out in their full finery.

One burial was outstanding and must have been for a person of great importance. The Bush Barrow contained two, and possibly three, daggers with highly decorated hilts, an axe, together with two diamond-shaped gold

clasps, probably for fastening cloaks across the chest, and a superb gold belt-hook cover. These gold items were decorated with fine parallel lines that enhanced the glitter of the gold. But most important of all, Bush Barrow also revealed a unique polished stone macehead. The macehead was fitted to the shaft by a bronze cap and the centre of the handle was decorated by three rings of carved zigzag bone inlay. None of the wooden shaft has survived, but it was probably about 45 centimetres (18 in) long. It is so elaborately decorated that there can be no doubt it was intended for ceremonial use, rather than as a club or weapon.

The Normanton Down group of barrows can be dated to about 1850–1700 BC, which would place them late in the Stonehenge sequence, towards the second part of Stage 4 – a period when, so far as we can tell, alterations at Stonehenge itself had ceased entirely.

One might imagine that in its very final stages, Stonehenge could produce no further surprises for its many modern admirers. But it has. They come in the form of over a hundred shallow prehistoric carvings on the surfaces of certain prominent stones. These images have given us an intriguing glimpse of the ceremonies and of the people that attended them, when Stonehenge was approaching the end of its long life as a popular shrine. In pre-literate societies, I believe carvings like these were the equivalents of actual polished stone axes two millennia previously. Perhaps they can best be thought of as the forerunners of the medieval and later memorials erected in Christian churches to men and women buried somewhere in the crypt or the graveyard. But in the case of Stonehenge, most of the graves lie beneath barrows, like Bush Barrow, out in the landscape surrounding the Stones.

It has long been known that many of the stones at Stonehenge carry carvings left there, as souvenirs of their visits, by tourists in the recent and not-so-recent past.[113] Then came a most remarkable revelation.

Around teatime on a summer's afternoon in early July 1953, Professor Richard Atkinson was preparing to photograph an unusual seventeenth-century inscription (by someone called Johannes Ludovicus) on Stone 53, of the southern pair of Trilithons.[114] The angle of the sunlight was perfect and he was about to take the picture, when suddenly his gaze fell on some much shallower carvings beneath and around the man's name. It must have been a magical moment. Immediately he recognized them as an Early Bronze Age dagger and several flat axes, all with their curved blades facing upwards.

This discovery triggered a search for more carvings and in the following years some forty-four were discovered. The recent laser-scan survey by Historic England has revealed another seventy-one axe-head carvings, giving a grand total of known axe-head carvings of 115.[115] In addition Stonehenge has revealed three carvings of bronze daggers. By far the majority of carvings are representations of flat axes,* in a huge variety, most of which can be closely matched by finds of actual metalwork, now in museum collections.[116] The largest group of axe carvings was found on the exterior face of Stone 4 of the Sarsen Circle, which revealed no less than fifty-nine examples. The carvings were all found low down on the stones, within reach of a standing or sitting person. None are found below the ground, which proves that they were made after the uprights had been erected. This is confirmed by the date range of the actual metal objects they represent, which is spread over the years 1750–1500 BC – some 700 years after the erection of the Sarsen Circle and the Trilithon Horseshoe.[117]

Stonehenge has revealed by far the largest collection of axe and dagger carvings in Britain, but others are known in Dorset and Scotland. All are found on stones belonging to tombs of various sorts.[118] So a link with death seems assured.

It was suggested earlier that the metalwork carvings might represent individuals or individual events, rather like carved memorials in churches. The great variety of axe shapes is remarkable and no attempt has been made

_____

* Flat axes are typical of the Early Bronze Age, prior to 1500 BC. After that date axes are made in very different shapes.

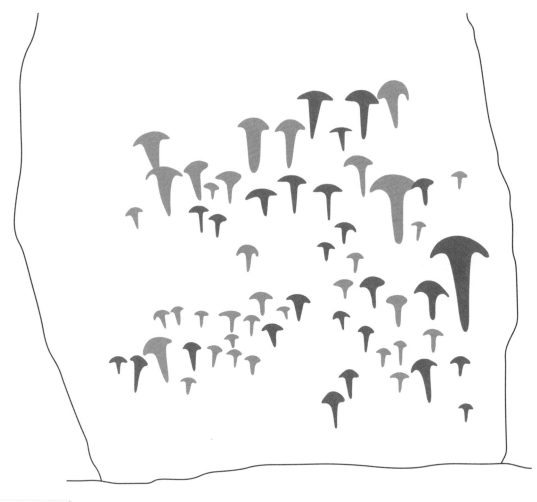

Rock Art

Discovered pre 2003

Discovered in 2012

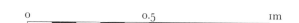

0   0.5   1m

Stonehenge Axe-head Carvings

to somehow standardize the representations. This was a time when metalwork was still relatively new and we know for a fact that high-quality metal objects were buried with important people. We also know from the toolmarks preserved on the timbers at Seahenge that at this period a large variety of axes were in use at the same time.[119] To modern eyes these axes all look vaguely similar, but to Early Bronze Age people every axe would soon have acquired its own identity – just as cars, bicycles or smartphones do today.

The sheer, and seemingly deliberate, variability of the axe and dagger carvings might suggest that they were the Bronze Age equivalents of medieval coats of arms, which instantly proclaimed the identity of individual knights during battle. Then later, in peacetime, the designs from the shields were placed over the fireplaces of great houses. Finally, they appeared in church memorials where they proclaimed the identity of the departed person. In a society where literacy was not universal, young men were trained to identify hundreds of coats of arms. I would suggest that something similar may have been happening when the axe and dagger carvings were made either during or just after, the funeral ceremonies at Stonehenge. Put another way, the carvings are shaped like axes and daggers, but they represent individuals and events. They tell us that Stonehenge was being used right up to its quite rapid demise in the years after 1500 BC. They also say something about the social status of the people who used Stonehenge in its final years. These were members of the elite. Its end may have been near, but there was to be no sad decline into oblivion. Stonehenge was going down with its reputation undiminished.

The exterior surface of Stone 4 of the Sarsen Circle revealed 59 carvings of Early Bronze Age flat axes, all with their curved cutting-edges facing upwards.

[overleaf]
A photograph of Stonehenge at sunrise.

8

AFTER THE STONES

Fields and farms of the
Stonehenge landscape in
the Late Bronze Age
(1300–800 BC). The round
barrows in the background
date to the Early Bronze
Age and were constructed
prior to 1500 BC.
Illustration by Jane Brayne.

The demise of Stonehenge coincides with perhaps the most significant change in religious and social behaviour in British prehistory. I have called this period of change the Domestic Revolution, because it was marked by a rapid shift away from large religious shrines, such as Stonehenge, that drew their worshippers from often quite distant places, to a new network of smaller, local sacred sites. Very often these new places were situated besides rivers, bogs, lakes, streams and springs. This change in religious emphasis was well underway by 1500 BC (it may have begun in certain places as early as 1700 BC[120]) and it was complete by 1400 BC. Essentially the new rites were based around the offering of objects, both commonplace and valuable, to the waters. The rites of what I have termed the New Order continued throughout prehistory and were thriving when the Romans arrived in AD 43. These Iron Age (after 800 BC) rituals, plus the artwork included in them, have subsequently been labelled as Celtic.

The religious rites of the New Order were by no means a complete break with what had gone before. The new shrines were places where the lives of the recently departed were commemorated. The alignment on sunrise moved from tombs and henges to the houses of the living, whose doorways would nearly always face southeast. The layout of many field systems respected the movement of the summer sun from east to west. But by 1500 BC the landscape of Britain had become developed: there were no longer huge expanses of woodland or rough scrub.

By 2000 BC field systems were starting to develop quite widely in lowland landscapes, and by 1500 BC the process was well advanced.[121] In places where fields did not (yet) exist, the landscape was already divided up using permanent markers, such as barrows or cairns and strategically sited rock carvings. Many river names in Britain, such as the Thames, have Celtic origins, which may well reflect their ancient role as boundaries.[122] Aerial photographs show that during the Bronze and Iron Ages, Britain was served by an elaborate system of roads and tracks.

Given such a developed landscape, local networks were bound to gain in importance and vast sites like Stonehenge that required long-distance travel ceased to be so attractive. Viewed from a long-term perspective, around 1500 BC British prehistory moved quite sharply from a developing phase (which in turn had grown from the Mesolithic pioneering phase) into a developed phase in which far-away contacts no longer needed to be ritually observed.[123] Put another way, the necessity to maintain long-distance social cohesion had passed. Societies were becoming more integrated as the general population grew; regional communities had learnt to live together. Solid evidence for tribal warfare and conflict, on anything approaching a large scale, is remarkably rare in later prehistoric Britain. The Iron Age is, however, well known for the construction of many hillforts. Unfortunately, the term 'hillfort' is very misleading, as by implication it suggests the tribes of Britain were constantly at war with each other. In actual fact, most hillforts were tribal centres that were probably built more to impress local communities than to deter enemies. Many, too, were not built in hilly country at all – like Vespasian's Camp, the nearest hillfort to Stonehenge, which was constructed in the fifth to fourth centuries BC.[124]

After 1500 BC the ceremonial journey from the land of the living to the realm of the ancestors had become a thing of the past. The Stonehenge ritual landscape was changing rapidly. What had once been a vast cemetery had now become a new land for the living. Fields were set out; crops were tilled and livestock grazed.

Now one might expect that the first fields to appear in a landscape would be very small scale and be positioned more or less at random around one or two farms. But that was not what happened. Britain can boast some of the earliest field systems in northern Europe, and like nearly all of them, the new fields around Stonehenge were laid out in an organized and coherent manner.[125] This would have involved not just one or two farmers but entire communities, as the fields were positioned to offer each landholder (usually a family) some of the best, some of the average and some of the worst-quality land. This often meant that fields were elongated and ran at right-angles to rivers and their flood plains. Very often – and this happened in the Stonehenge landscape – fields were aligned on barrows, which would suggest that the initial layout took place in the Early Bronze Age, when such monuments were still being respected.[126] It also links the management of land to earlier arrangements where open grazing would have been parcelled up between different families, whose territories, or holdings, were separated by burial mounds. The ancestors were universally respected and their presence within the mounds would have been symbolically very important. So the fields that followed the Stones did not appear 'out of the blue': they were part of a continuing process of landscape change that ultimately reflected the needs of a steadily increasing population.

Even with the takeover by the new farms and fields of the previous ritual landscape, the great monument of Stonehenge itself could not be completely ignored. Finds of later Bronze Age pottery are not unusual.[127] Iron Age pottery has been found in the higher layers of many features.[128] Even pottery of the Roman period is quite often found in layers that have accumulated naturally over time (in other words, they have not been deliberately back-filled) – for example, in the upper filling of the Aubrey Holes.[129] Moving forward in time, Saxon pottery has been found in the naturally accumulated filling of the mysterious Phase 5 Y and Z Holes – along with many other sherds of Roman and even medieval date.[130] And this brings us to the early origin of the name 'Stonehenge', which is generally believed to have been derived from two Early English words (*stan* + *hengen*), which literally mean 'stone' and 'hanging'.[131] Many people have since jumped to the conclusion that the 'hanging' is a reference to the Stones' superficial resemblance to a gallows. Today, however, most opinion would prefer to see the 'hanging' as an allusion to the fact that the lintels appear to be hanging in the air.[132]

We will discuss some of the many ways that Stonehenge has affected the millions of people who have visited it over the years in the final chapter. Here we are still considering the actual physical remains of the monument and how they fared after 1500 BC. So we will conclude with some thoughts on the varied impacts that all sorts of visitors have had on the Stones. It is still not unusual to see pictures in the press of modern Druids and others attending rituals there on the midsummer solstice. But what damage have they inflicted? And what about the upsurge of new fields and farms in later prehistory: did their builders use Stonehenge as a quarry for stone? And finally, what about the well-meaning efforts of archaeologists: how much have they – have we – disturbed the site by their excavations?

Like many great achievements of architects and engineers, Stonehenge was built to impress. And just like builders of the recent past, the people who erected the great Stones did so at the expense of their foundations. It was essential, for example, to get the lintels of the Sarsen Circle to sit as high as possible, yet be absolutely level. One result of this was that many of the stone-holes were too shallow, and once a few vertical stones had shifted, lintels then toppled and uprights soon followed.[133] Today we have grown used to insensitive restorations or 'improvements' to old buildings, but people were just as capable of seemingly idiotic decisions in prehistory. In Stage 3, just a century or so after the erection of the Sarsen Circle and the magnificent Trilithon Horseshoe, it was decided to dig a deep pit at the very base of the Great Trilithon.[134] Nobody knows why this was done, but in due course it led to the Trilithon's collapse.[135]

The subsequent history of Stonehenge is a sorry tale, but probably no worse than any other prominent ancient monument. As we can still see at the ruins of places like the great Cistercian abbeys of Yorkshire, later generations can be blind to the most glorious architectural achievements of their predecessors. The comprehensive round-up of research at Stonehenge, published by English Heritage in 1995, devoted an entire chapter to the details of what it described as 'Post-Bronze Age Use and Abuse'. Some of this work was done to prevent further decay and collapse[136] – the majority of the standing stones, for example, were straightened in the twentieth century and several were re-erected.[137]

While patient research in museum archives can provide fascinating insights into the way people have used, abused and cared for ancient sites, the places themselves also carry tell-tale evidence that can now be revealed, thanks to laser scanning. We saw in the previous chapter how the Historic England laser-scan survey had more than doubled the number of known Early Bronze Age carvings on the Stones, but it was also able to reveal evidence of damage – some of it very subtle, some quite blatant.[138]

Good research should never be over-focused and the laser-scan was no exception, as it also involved a careful examination of the state of each and every stone at Stonehenge. This survey concluded that most of the stones that had been standing since their erection in prehistory were either complete or near-complete. By contrast most of the stones that had collapsed had either been split or damaged. This might have happened in the fall, but of the six stones whose fall has been recorded in history, only one, a lintel, had been damaged when it fell. There is, however, good evidence that large parts of at least eight fallen stones have been taken away from the site. The survey suggests that the five missing uprights of the Sarsen Circle had once been there, but had subsequently been removed – most probably in fragments.[139] These large pieces of stone would probably have been reshaped and used in houses or farm buildings.

While the Sarsen Circle seems to have fared poorly, the stones of the Trilithon Horseshoe appear to be substantially complete, even if the collapsed stones have suffered quite badly by being walked over and damaged by visitors. Many of the stones of the Bluestone Circle, like those of the Sarsen Circle alongside them, have been damaged, broken or removed, but the Bluestone Horseshoe, within the Trilithon Horseshoe, is largely complete.

William Gowland (wearing
a cap, *second from left*)
supervises digging around
stone 56 at Stonehenge,
1901.

Visitors have caused damage, sometimes unwittingly with their feet,
other times more deliberately by carving their names. The laser survey
revealed forty-four examples of prominent graffiti, but hundreds of smaller
scratched names were also detected. The architect of St. Paul's Cathedral,
London, Sir Christopher Wren ('I WREN'), left his name on the Trilithon
upright, Stone 52.

Another major cause of damage was the removal of souvenir chips
of stone to take home as mementos. This appalling practice reached a
peak in the nineteenth century when a correspondent to *The Times*
newspaper in 1871 complained that his visit to Stonehenge was spoiled by
the din of people hammering at the stones for souvenirs.[140] More recently
the wear caused by shoes standing on collapsed stones has removed much
surface information, such as evidence for their shaping, and any shallow
carvings. It is hard to believe, but people have even lit barbecue fires
against the stones.[141] Stone chips continued occasionally to be removed
until the site was fenced off to visitors in 1978. The last recorded damage of
this sort was reported in 2008 when a vandal removed a chip from the Heel
Stone.[142]

We must conclude this general catalogue of woe with a very brief review
of the damage that has been inflicted on Stonehenge by archaeologists. The
great archaeologist Sir Mortimer Wheeler famously stated: 'At the best,
excavation is destruction.'[143] He went on to point out that the only thing that
distinguished excavation from methodical destruction was the fact that a
detailed report was produced at the end of the process. Sadly, this did not
always happen at Stonehenge. Indeed, two of the principal excavators of
Stonehenge have left us short interim statements – written at the conclusion
of each season's excavations – and even popular books on the subject, but no
proper, in-depth, fully illustrated final reports. Even their notes and diaries
made in the field are thin and not always very informative. Over the past
forty or so years the authorities controlling access to Stonehenge have hugely
tightened up their procedures and such abuses are not likely to occur again.

But we must publicly acknowledge that they did happen, and make sure they are *never* repeated.

The story of modern research into Stonehenge began in an exemplary fashion with the excavations in 1901 of Professor William Gowland.[144] He only opened a few small trenches close to Stone 56, but in many ways was years ahead of his time, meticulously recording every find in three dimensions – something that is much easier to do with today's satellite surveying technology. He also published his research fully and promptly the following year.[145]

After the Great War it was realized that many of the leaning uprights had to be straightened or reinforced and that the various wooden poles that had been used to prop them up since the nineteenth century were unsightly and inadequate. Excavations ahead of this work began in 1919 and continued until 1926 under the direction of Lt.-Col. William Hawley. This extended project excavated over half the total area of the ditch and a substantial portion of the southeastern interior. The project was carried out on a shoestring budget and Hawley's health suffered as a result of the working conditions. For at least the first season he was accompanied by a competent local archaeologist, Robert Newall, who helped with the drawings and recording processes, but soon he had to be dropped owing to financial constraints. The actual quality of the on-site recording has been described as 'of a reasonable high standard for the time'.[146] Having said that, the site was Stonehenge, so one might have expected better, especially given the fact that the project was supervised and officially controlled by no less than the Society of Antiquaries of London and the Ministry of Works.[147] The project's written records essentially consist of Hawley's daily dairies, which have subsequently been typed out and copied. Plans were drawn by visiting Ministry of Works draftsmen and are reasonably good.[148] His excavation records are coherent and all finds are recorded to a foot square, with a depth, and there is also a good photographic archive. The better finds have been preserved in Salisbury Museum and the British Museum, but everything else

Two boys get up to no good on a school trip to Stonehenge in the 1950s.

was reburied in 'Hawley's Graves' – ten pits dug near his site hut to the south of the site. But there was no final report. Instead, we have been left with seven interim accounts published in the *Antiquaries Journal* at the end of each season, from 1921 to 1928. Typically these are about twenty pages long. They are certainly better than nothing, especially given the quality of the surviving site archive, but they do contain errors.[149] Normally speaking, one would expect an excavation of this importance and longevity to have been published in several fat volumes, each of 500 pages or more.

The next major series of excavations were carried out after the Second World War, between 1950 and 1964. The work was directed by three eminent archaeologists (two of them professors), with the aim of resolving problems raised by Hawley's work. Latterly the project was involved with the straightening of a leaning Trilithon. The records kept were inadequate, even by Hawley's earlier standards. Indeed, the 1995 summary of work carried out at Stonehenge in the twentieth century is damning in its understatement: 'No written site records have been found from the 1950–64 excavations, and it seems that none were produced.'[150] Plans and drawings were so inadequate that it was impossible even to compare depths with Hawley's earlier work. Apart from a short interim statement on the very early research into two Aubrey Holes (in 1952), no report was ever published.[151] The only published information on fourteen seasons of excavation is the popular (and very good) account by Professor Atkinson, which first appeared in 1956, and was revised in 1979.[152]

There have been other smaller excavations, of which the later examples were published, but we still lack any records for at least two projects (1922 and 1927) on the Stonehenge Avenue. Work from 1967 onwards has been to a high standard, with full reports, records and archives.

It is probably fair to say that Stonehenge has fared worse at the hands of archaeologists than any other major British site. That said, the landmark publication of *Stonehenge in its Landscape: Twentieth Century Excavations* (1995) has been a monumental and valiant attempt by Wessex Archaeology and English

Heritage to salvage something from the disgraceful catalogue of failures of so many high-profile excavations in the recent past.[153] That publication gave us accurate plans and, where possible, sections, plus numerous photographs. Perhaps its biggest achievement has been the creation of the Wessex Archaeology Stonehenge Archive, which is housed in Salisbury Museum.[154]

But to conclude on an optimistic note, recent research has produced a wealth of promptly published accurate, information that is transforming our understanding of this extraordinary monument. Stonehenge is now receiving its due: imaginative research and scholarly interpretation. Special efforts have been made to shape future research.[155] This new work will make sure that the Stones continue to colour and inspire Britain's identity in a changing world. So the final chapter will investigate how this extraordinary prehistoric site on Salisbury Plain has fuelled the creativity of artists, writers and film-makers over the past 400 years.

[overleaf]
Stonehenge at Sunset, 1836 by John Constable (1776–1837).

9

STONEHENGE TODAY

Stonehenge is an icon. This is a much over-used word in the twenty-first century, especially in its adjectival form, 'iconic', which today means little more than extra-special, or even eye-catching, especially if featured on a celebrity. But an icon, in its original sense, was a special Christian painting, often of the Holy Family, which was believed to have supernatural, sometimes miraculous, properties.[156] Essentially an icon was about more than the subject it represented. Today images of Stonehenge have been used to sell everything from rock band albums, such as *Stonedhenge* by Ten Years After (1969), to England as a tourist destination. But of course there is far more to it than that.

The many ways that people have studied, thought about and portrayed Stonehenge have intrigued a variety of scholars over the past 300 years, but until Christopher Chippindale's remarkable *Stonehenge Complete* (1983) nobody had attempted to synthesize and draw them all together.[157] In many important respects this book complements the comprehensive review of the archaeological evidence produced by English Heritage twelve years later.[158]

Many artists have fallen under the spell of Stonehenge. Admittedly it was easier in the days when one could walk through and beneath the great hanging stones, but even from their periphery the modern visitor can still sense their extraordinary presence. They seem to stand for time itself, and the more we learn about their transport, shaping, construction and modification, the more wonderful they become. As a symbol of human achievement, Stonehenge is uniquely perfect – and that perfection was achieved without reading or writing and probably, too, without the controlling eye of an architectural genius. In that important respect Stonehenge differs profoundly from other great icons of art or architecture, such as St Peter's in Rome, Versailles or, closer to home, Blenheim Palace. It represents the collective consciousness of illiterate communities over many generations. And yet the end result is close to perfection.

Visitors have long been moved by the Stones. Celia Fiennes (1662–1741) was a pioneering traveller and tourist who visited most large English country houses and places of note in her journeys of the late seventeenth and early eighteenth centuries. She kept diaries and wrote memoirs, which were eventually fully published in 1947.[159] Her account gives a revealing insight into what an educated visitor would have thought at the time.[160] She is remarkably observant and is struck by the fact that Stonehenge sits within a landscape rich in ancient remains.[161] She also notices that the lintels were secured in place by mortice holes and that there are a distinct category of smaller stones. She remarks on the great hardness of sarsen and even wonders whether it was a concrete-like artificial stone. There was also a myth at the time that nobody could count the stones of Stonehenge twice and reach the same total. She did so – and arrived at ninety-one each time, which is probably fairly accurate for the time.

Other, and later, visitors to Stonehenge have been less rational. A very influential figure in what one might term the 'alternative view' of landscape history has been Alfred Watkins, whose book, *The Old Straight Track* (1925), offered a semi-mystical re-imagining of the way the British landscape took shape. In the past this book was regarded by most academics as quite simply mad, but today we are less inclined to make such harsh judgements. As a recent editor wisely remarked, having pointed out some of the book's many factual shortcomings: 'Watkins re-enchanted the English landscape, investing it with fresh depth and detail, prompting new ways of looking and new reasons to walk.'[162] Watkins's idea was that Stone Age people would find their way through the untamed wilderness by walking in straight lines towards prominent markers, usually on the skyline. These lines he called leys or ley lines, and as time passed ancient sites accumulated around and along them. We now know that there is an archaeological site in almost every square quarter mile of Britain, so it is

Foamhenge: a view of the sarsen circle from the north-east, showing the Great Trilithon in the background. Also note the guy-ropes: the Styrofoam 'stones' would start to move in a light, Force 3, breeze.

hardly surprising that some can be linked by straight lines. We also know that the story of prehistoric landscape development is vastly more complex than a series of lines. Nevertheless, his ideas did inspire many to take an active interest in landscape history at a time when most families had more leisure and the countryside was being opened up for (and by) people from the rapidly expanding cities and suburbs.

Watkins believed that Stonehenge was placed at the junction of three distinct ley lines, one of which followed the midsummer sunrise, and the Avenue (then newly discovered); another was on the lunar alignment marked by the North and South Barrows and their Station Stones.[163] The problem with Watkins's and similar approaches is that they treat the landscape as a blank canvas, which it never was. As we have seen in this book, sites like Stonehenge can only be adequately appreciated if we take everything into account. Lines and alignments played a role, but they were only a small part of what was to become an extraordinarily complex story.

Paintings of Stonehenge can reveal much about an artist's approach and inspiration. The great architect Inigo Jones studied Roman architecture in Italy and designed one of the first classical buildings in London, St. Paul's Church, Covent Garden (which is still standing and well worth a visit). It is said to be based on the proportions he observed at Stonehenge, which he believed to have been a Roman creation. His ideas were published in 1655, shortly after his death, and they included a wonderfully 'rationalized' version of Stonehenge as if it had been created by architects who followed the plain, early Roman Tuscan Order of architecture.[164] To reach such symmetrical perfection, Jones introduced an additional Trilithon.

Stonehenge has been painted by many artists from at least the sixteenth century, but two of the most memorable depictions were by British painters of world renown. The first is by John Constable. It is based on a pencil sketch made on his only visit to the site on 15 July 1820, which still survives, as does another sketch drawn in the studio in 1822. Two watercolours were then developed from the initial sketches, before the final painting was produced,

some fifteen years after the artist had visited the site. At its public exhibition, Constable added an explanatory note that gives us a clear idea of what made him choose Stonehenge as a subject: 'The mysterious monument of Stonehenge, standing remote on a bare and boundless heath, as much unconnected with the events of past ages as it is with the uses of the present, carries you back beyond all historical recall into the obscurity of a totally unknown period.'[165]

The second notable early-nineteenth-century painting is a watercolour by J. M. W. Turner. It appeared in 1828 and no preliminary sketches or working drawings have survived. As a pictorial record of the monument, it is far less accurate than the Constable painting, but what it lacks in accuracy it more than makes up in drama. The turbulent sky, complete with a descending thunderbolt, seems to have cut down the waking ewes and their two-month-old lambs in the foreground. Meanwhile their shepherd sleeps on, seemingly dead to the rapidly approaching storm. The picture caused much interest at the time; indeed, the great art critic, John Ruskin described it as 'the standard of storm-drawing'.[166]

There have been numerous other representations of Stonehenge, but none can be compared with the two extraordinary paintings by Turner and Constable, which still continue to influence the way people imagine the site. But by the later twentieth century new processes and techniques had arisen that gave artists and film-makers the opportunity to represent Stonehenge in sometimes unexpected ways. Over the midsummer solstice of 2005 I had the good fortune to be asked to appear on a 'live' television documentary to be made for Channel 5. It would involve a full-size recreation of Stonehenge, but made from coloured Styrofoam blocks. Inevitably it became widely known as 'Foamhenge'. At first I thought it must be a joke, but when I arrived on set my doubts were immediately dispelled. The reconstruction was meticulously accurate, thanks to the advice of the former curator of Avebury Museum, Dr Mike Pitts. The replica 'Foamhenge', although somewhat exaggerated, does clearly show the contrast between the two types of stone used. The bluestones and sarsens are represented as if they had been freshly quarried, when their natural colours would have been brightest. Despite being feather-light, the Styrofoam 'stones' somehow gave the recreated monument an extraordinary presence and air of reality. In the end it proved a profoundly moving experience, and one I will never forget.

The second example of a Stonehenge recreation in a modern medium is the well-known bouncy castle version, named *Sacrilege*, which was created by Turner Prize-winning artist Jeremy Deller to celebrate the opening of the 2012 London Olympics. In July of that year we welcomed it to the Bronze Age site at Flag Fen, Peterborough, where it was inflated in a grass meadow that lay directly above the earliest known field system in England. That field system came into being around 2500 BC, the date when the great stones were erected at faraway Stonehenge.

Jeremy Deller's *Sacrilege*, shortly after inflation at Flag Fen. Note the Sarsen Circle, *left*, and elements of the Trilithon Horseshoe, *right*.

Perhaps the most important development in the modern story of Stonehenge has been the closing of the A344 road and the construction of a new Visitor Centre further away from the Stones, 1½ miles (2 km) to the northwest (at the junction of the A360 and B3086 roads). The opening of the new centre and the closure of the A344 marks an important milestone in Stonehenge's development, as it allows the site to be appreciated within a wider landscape, free from the clutter of buildings, cars and coaches. The next

STONEHENGE TODAY

stage will be the concealing and silencing of the nearby A303 trunk road in a tunnel; only when that is complete will its setting finally be worthy of a World Heritage Site.[167]

The new Visitor Centre, a striking building in its own right, was designed by architects Denton Corker Marshall, and opened in December 2013. By the same time the following year the site had welcomed 1.3 million visitors – a 9 per cent increase on the previous year. They included President Barack Obama, who came in September – and was allowed to walk around the centre of the site. The new Visitor Centre includes displays and photographs of ancient objects found on and near the site, but it is particularly notable for the reconstructed houses of the Durrington Walls settlement (see Chapter 6). The outside display also features a replica of an upright from the Sarsen Circle, resting on a timber sledge, as if being transported. Visitors can push the sledge to gain an impression of what 20 tonnes feels like. They can also appreciate the sheer scale of the great stones, which is not so evident at a distance.

Recent research has taken us a long way down the winding road that leads to a rounded appreciation of both Stonehenge and the people who built it. But will we ever fully understand what was going through their minds as they manhandled 20-ton rocks across the Marlborough Downs? Put another way, why on earth did they decide to build it? We have tried to address that question in this book. Yes, we undoubtedly know much more about Neolithic societies and what motivated them than we did even twenty years ago. But have we arrived at the whole truth? Sadly, that is a question that even the most meticulous excavation will never be able to answer.

At the Stonehenge Visitor Centre visitors can try to push a full-weight replica of one of the Sarsen Circle uprights, as it might have appeared during its journey to Stonehenge around 2500 BC.

[overleaf]
Stonehenge, 1835, by John Constable (1776–1837). This oil painting was exhibited at the Royal Academy in 1836.

APPENDIX I

TIMELINE OF SIGNIFICANT EVENTS
IN BRITISH PREHISTORY

A Prospect of STONE-HENGE From the west

A Prospect of STONE-HENGE From the south

NOTE: This timeline provides some key dates in later British prehistory as a chronological setting for the story of Stonehenge. A small number of important dates elsewhere in the world are also included (in *italic* type).

*c.*10,900 BC
Start of the final cold phase of the Ice Age.
Glaciers start to reform in upland parts of Scotland, Wales and England.

*c.*10,500 BC
Start of Japanese Jomon pottery tradition.

*c.*10,000 BC
Earliest agriculture begins in Iran.

*c.*9000 BC
Earliest agriculture begins in India.

*c.*8000 BC
Potatoes farmed in the Andean region of South America.

*c.*9600 BC
Climate warms by ten degrees Celsius in just 50 years. Sea levels rise.

*c.*9400 BC
Humans return to Britain, then joined to continental Europe.

*c.*9300–8400 BC
Star Carr Mesolithic site (North Yorkshire) first occupied by this date.

*c.*8000 BC
Building of the walls of Jericho.

*c.*6500 BC
Britain becomes an island, due to continuously rising sea levels.

*c.*6200 BC
Massive tsunami floods Norway, parts of Scotland and northern England.

*c.*5500 BC
First causewayed enclosures built in continental Europe.

*c.*4200 BC
Arrival of farming in Britain. End of the Mesolithic.

*c.*4000 BC
The ancestor to modern maize farmed in Mesoamerica.

*c.*4000–3500 BC
The Early Neolithic period in Britain.

*c.*3900–3800 BC
Construction of first megalithic tombs in Britain.

*c.*3800–3600 BC
Main construction phase for long barrows in Britain.

*c.*3800–3400 BC
Construction and use of causewayed enclosures in Britain.

c.3500–2900 BC
The Middle Neolithic period in Britain.

c.3200 BC
Construction of the great chambered tomb of Newgrange, Ireland.

c.3200–1600 BC
Era of stone circles in Britain.

c.2900–2500 BC
The Late Neolithic period in Britain.

c.3200–2800 BC
Construction of early, or formative, henges.

c.2900–1800 BC
Construction of classic henges.

c.2500–2200 BC
The British Copper Age, or Chalcolithic.

c.2200–1500 BC
The Early Bronze Age.

c.2000 BC
Field systems are constructed in Britain.

c.1600–1046 BC
Shang Dynasty in China.

c.1500 BC
Barrows, henges and ritual landscapes decline rapidly.

1332–1323 BC
Reign of Pharaoh Tutankhamun of Egypt.

c.1500–1000 BC
The Middle Bronze Age.

c.1000–8/700 BC
The Late Bronze Age.

c.1000 BC
The first hillforts are constructed.

c.8/700 BC – AD 43
The Iron Age.

476–221 BC
Great Wall of China built during the period of the Warring States.

55 and 54 BC
Julius Caesar's two campaigns in Britain.

AD 43
Roman troops under the Emperor Claudius invade Britain. Prehistory ends.

APPENDIX II

THE DITCH AND THE GRADUAL ESTABLISHMENT OF STONEHENGE

[previous page]
A picnic party at Stone-
henge in 1877. The group
include Queen Victoria's
son Prince Leopold, Duke
of Albany, who reclines on
the ground, *fifth from left*.

We saw in Chapter 4 that it is currently accepted that the first significant development in the immediate area of Stonehenge was the digging of the enclosing ditch and its accompanying banks. Today the ditch can still be seen as a shallow depression, which surrounds the Stones and marks the edge of the monument. The digging of the ditch is currently interpreted as a single event that radiocarbon dates indicate took place around 3000–2900 BC – a date that marks the start of Stonehenge Stage 1. These dates are based on samples taken from the ditch. It is this interpretation and dating that will be addressed in this appendix.

Normally radiocarbon samples from the bottom of a ditch would accurately reflect when it was dug. But we will suggest below that the Stonehenge ditch was not a 'normal' prehistoric ditch, because its inspiration lay in a much earlier tradition of monuments, known as causewayed enclosures, which we described in Chapter 3. The ditches surrounding these earlier Neolithic enclosures – and many have been excavated in Britain and Europe – are characterized by frequent redigging or re-cutting. It will be suggested here that the currently accepted radiocarbon dates for the Stonehenge ditch refer to the latest stages of its redigging. Other, purely archaeological evidence will be used to make a case that the initial laying out of the monument did not happen in a single event, but probably took place over almost half a millennium, starting around, or possibly even shortly before, 3300 BC.

It could be argued that the new ditch, being the earliest major feature on the site, would provide clear evidence not just for the date, but for the way Stonehenge was used prior to the erection of the Stones. Unfortunately, however, more than half of the ditch was completely excavated between 1919 and 1926, using workmen and techniques that would not be employed today. Very few drawings were made of the 'sections' or layers of soil encountered in the ditch, although the few that were done were to a high standard. But the excavator, Lt.-Col William

Hawley, did keep quite a comprehensive daily diary, which the compilers of the report into Stonehenge research in the twentieth century have used for their substantial reassessment of the earlier work.[168] Their detailed account provides good evidence that the digging and filling in of the ditch followed a similar pattern to that observed at modern excavations of causewayed enclosure ditches elsewhere in Britain. Indeed, Hawley would have been aware of such work, as Alexander Keiller's excavations were taking place at Windmill Hill, near Avebury, just 20 miles to the north, from 1925.[169]

There is always a danger, especially when comparing sites from different regions, of allowing what are assumed to be significant similarities, or differences, to become too detailed. In such situations the devil rarely lies in the detail – and generally, broad comparisons work the best. So when I came to examine the published records for Hawley's excavation of the ditch, I was immediately reminded of what we had observed in the later ditch deposits of the Etton causewayed enclosure (see Chapter 3). But something was not quite right: there seemed to be an inconsistency.

We saw in Chapter 3 that the causewayed ditch at Etton was characterized by a series of offerings or 'placed' deposits, which we believe may have symbolized events in a family or clan's history. These offerings changed both in style and layout over the two centuries or so of the site's main use. We could identify four quite distinct phases, which could clearly be distinguished in the ground.[170] More recently a reassessment of the radiocarbon dates of British causewayed enclosures has clearly shown that the first three phases (1A–C) at Etton were quite short-lived, but also formed a close but neatly separated sequence that evolved without any breaks. It is a remarkably precise sequence.[171] Each of the three sub-phases of Phase 1 probably lasted for about half a century, or two to three generations, at most.

The final phase (2) at Etton took place a century or two after the primary three phases, but its duration is harder to pin down using radiocarbon dates alone. The archaeological evidence suggests that this later phase represents more episodic or occasional use of the site than had been the case in Phase 1.

The Etton causewayed enclosure lies low in the floodplain of the River Welland, at the point where it merges into the East Anglian Fens. Sea levels were slightly lower in the fourth millennium BC than today, but the Fens had started to form and the landscape around Etton was being subjected to regular flooding, especially in winter. Ground water levels were gradually rising, and this may help to explain why the three successive deposits of Phases 1 A–C survived so intact. It would also explain why the site had been completely abandoned by 3000 BC and ritual activity transferred along the Maxey Cursus to the Maxey Henge, higher on the natural gravel island of Maxey.

The ditch at Etton seems to have been first dug by relatively small groups of people. In some segments the ditch plan and profile is quite regular, which might suggest it was recut quite often. In other areas the lower profile is very scooped and irregular, which would suggest that quite small parties – families perhaps – were at work.[172] The lower levels of the Stonehenge ditch seem to be similarly varied, and the undulating or lobed areas are, if anything, even more pit-like and irregular.[173] Again, this would indicate small working parties.

The offerings, or 'placed' deposits, belonging to Phase 1A at Etton consisted of a series of quite distinct heaps, separated by spaces. These heaps were placed in a row along the freshly dug bottom of the ditch. They included complete pottery vessels, bones from feasting, human skulls, and many other combinations of bone, pottery, flint and antler. Although it was sometimes hard to be precise, it did seem that the isolated heaped offerings along the ditch bottom corresponded with individual lobes in the initial digging of the ditch. The arrangement of offerings to coincide with undulations and re-cuts occasionally continued into the second phase (1B) and was particularly evident in one segment of ditch, where fragments of broken quernstone were placed at the edges of lobes, in a three-lobed ditch segment.[174] After each series of offerings had been made, the ditch was then filled in with the gravel that had been dug from it. In general, the second, Phase 1B, re-cutting of the ditch was less deep, but more regular in profile. The two episodes of re-cutting that went with the offerings of Phases 1B and 1C stopped short of the earliest, Phase 1A, deposits. This may have been deliberate, or it might have been a result of rising water levels.

In the final primary phase (1C), the irregularities of the initial digging had been filled in and a new series of offerings were made in the bottom of the re-cut ditch. This re-cut was narrower and shallower than the others and the offerings were now placed in a central row, with less distinctly defined 'heaps', although it was sometimes possible to identify clearly individual offerings or events.[175]

The general trend from clearly defined individual offerings (Phase 1A) to the line or row of continuous offerings (Phase 1C) was also characterized by miniaturization. Thus in Phase 1A human heads are represented by complete skulls, or by skull-sized upside-down round-bottom bowls.[176] But by Phase 1C, just over a century later, human heads were represented by fragments of bone, or in one case by a tennis-ball-sized and roughly carved fossil sea urchin.[177] Put briefly, the general trend is from separated and distinct individual offerings placed within a ditch that sometimes resembles a series of joined-up pits, to a series of smaller offerings placed in a continuous row, within a shallower recut ditch, whose shape is far more regular and ditch-like. And then, in Phase 2, there was another change.

By the late fourth millennium BC, Etton was becoming wetter and was not used as regularly as it had been in Phase 1. By now the ditches had been largely filled in, but we know they were still distinctly visible, and probably marked out by low banks, as at Stonehenge today. So the Phase 2 use of the ditch takes the form of a few narrow gully-like recuts, with offerings placed in loose groups, rather than rows. Alternatively, filled-in ditch segments were dug into by deep, pit-like re-cuts. These deeper re-cuts destroyed and disturbed the Phase 1 offerings beneath them. One of these pits had been used to bury the skull, complete with huge horns, of an aurochs (wild cattle).[178] These late offerings frequently include antler and antler fragments, plus pottery, as in Phase 1, but now a different style of vessel was being used.[179] The new style is known as Grooved Ware. It is found widely across the British Isles, and frequently at henges and other ceremonial sites from Orkney to Stonehenge, where it is only found in the ditch.[180] By way of contrast, the pottery found in the holes dug for the great standing stones and other features of Stages 1–5 is later in style.[181] Again, this suggests an earlier date for the re-cutting, if not for the actual digging of the ditch.

Although the excavation methods used in the early twentieth century were far from ideal, it has proved possible to isolate a number of likely offerings in the Stonehenge ditch. To the northwest of the main entrance (later approached by the Avenue), two deposits of antlers, which had been burnt *in situ* in the pit-like enlargements, were found at the bottom of the ditch. There were fewer finds on the other, southwestern side, but the excavator's diary makes reference to the horn and large bones of a 'bison' (probably an aurochs) on the bottom of the ditch.

Other offerings in the ditch include three groups of animal bone and a group of antlers halfway up the ditch filling.[182] There is also evidence that possible offerings had been disturbed in antiquity. An antler pick and chalk ball were found in secondary (i.e. not original) deposits, just off the ditch bottom in the enlargement of the ditch northwest of the main entrance.[183] Finally, a cremation was found *in situ*, lying directly on the ditch bottom.[184] This has to have been a placed deposit.

It is tempting to suggest that these are the sorts of things we might have discovered had we excavated the ditch at Etton with picks, mattocks and shovels, rather than the trowels and dental picks we employed. Each ditch segment at Etton took several months to excavate and all finds were recorded in three dimensions. It was very slow, painstaking work. The earlier (Phase 1) offerings at Etton could be very subtle indeed. And some, like a piece of flax twine or sheet of birch bark, would not have survived in the dry ground at Stonehenge. But there is evidence that similar, subtler deposits might once have existed there. The chalk balls are a good example: were these symbolic skulls, the equivalents of the Etton fossil sea urchin? Even given the few surviving section drawings, there can be little doubt that the ditch had been back-filled in antiquity, just as happened at Etton between each of the sub-phases.[185] Perhaps this was when much disturbance of the earlier deposits took place (this did not happen at Etton, possibly due to rising water levels).

The offerings in the Stonehenge ditch that have survived are entirely consistent with Etton Phase 2, especially as regards the cremation, the aurochs skull and the numerous finds of antler. Although there are exceptions, such as the two enlargements on either side of the main entrance, which were fashioned somewhat later, the lobed, almost sinuous, pit-like profile of the lower ditch in its southeastern lengths is highly reminiscent of Etton in its earliest phase.[186] One could select many parallels among excavated British causewayed enclosures, but the central ring of highly segmented ditches (the so-called 'spiral arm') at Briar Hill, Northampton, is also close in size and shape to the Stonehenge ditch.[187] If anything, the pit-like, lobed layout is even more pronounced there. Briar Hill was also particularly challenging to excavate because of its numerous complex re-cuttings, which (in common with the ditch) proved extremely difficult to correlate satisfactorily across the site.[188]

The initial digging of causewayed enclosure ditches is generally agreed to have been carried out by so-called 'gang-labour', which we have suggested is likely to have been based around the family, tribe or community. Such communal projects would have drawn widely from groups of people across a region. The work would have been a way of cementing far-flung communities together. Like modern rural livestock markets, they would also have had a social side, which we know involved feasting. Marriage arrangements made at such festivities would have fostered long-distance family ties, while also counteracting the inevitable tendency towards inbreeding. At first, the groups attending causewayed enclosures were quite small, to judge by the size of the short, pit-like extensions of many ditch segments. There are, moreover, no good reasons to suppose that the ditch was dug in one single 'event'. More likely its general course would have been agreed, but it was never meant to have been a single, unified feature, such as the great ditches that surround Iron Age hillforts or medieval castles. But as time passed, the groups became larger and better organized – and this is expressed by longer, re-cut, lengths of ditch. Over some four or five centuries, these working parties were to become large enough and sufficiently well co-ordinated to erect the massive uprights and lintels of Stonehenge.

I would suggest that the ditch at Stonehenge follows the practices and traditions that were current in the final stages of causewayed enclosures. These were rooted in an earlier family- or clan-based system of social organization, appropriate to the smaller, widely separated communities of the period 3700–3500 BC. By the middle of the fourth millennium BC these traditions had evolved. By this time tribes, rather than individual families, provided the workforce, which would have involved larger and better-organized gangs. If we assume that the first episodes of digging the Stonehenge ditch took place around 3300 BC (which would accord best with the available radiocarbon dates), then they would probably have followed earlier work practices, but with larger gangs than previously. The rites and ceremonies surrounding the initial digging of the ditch would have evolved from earlier traditions. So different segments of the ditch would have 'represented' individual tribes or communities. Individual segments would have been seen as of comparable importance to the ditch as a whole. Unlike modern archaeologists they would not necessarily have viewed the ditch as 'a monument'; their attitude would have been more complex – and ambivalent. There was also considerable autonomy, or independence, in the timing not just of the digging of different segments, but in their subsequent re-cutting. It probably took at least three centuries for the family or community-based organization of the labour force to evolve into something more centrally controlled. And maybe earlier conditions lingered even longer. For example, it is interesting that offerings were only made in the ditch to the west of the main entranceway. Had the work been more centrally controlled, one might have expected to find matching offerings on either side.

At first glance, the layout and segmented structure of the Stonehenge ditch do indeed closely resemble that of a causewayed enclosure. So could it have been dug when most of them came into being around 3700–3600 BC?[189] There are two principal objections to this. The first is that Neolithic pottery of this earlier period is very distinctive. Indeed, it must have been familiar to Hawley, because, as we have seen, the nearby enclosure at Windmill Hill was being excavated at the time he was digging the ditch. Even given the methods he employed, it is hard to believe he failed to recognize it entirely – and nor has any been found in subsequent work at Stonehenge.[190] The alignment of the ditch entranceway on the solstice is unique among causewayed enclosures, but it is very much a part of the newer, Middle Neolithic tradition represented by passage graves and henges, which began in the centuries after 3500 BC.[191] Having said that, of course, we do know that Stonehenge seems to have been carefully positioned in line with the distinctive subsoil grooves beneath the final stretch of the Avenue, and that these were probably recognized in Mesolithic times.

Sometime shortly before 3000 BC, a new dynamic had begun to take hold at Stonehenge. Maybe the complex series of events that surrounded the narrowing and near-blocking of the southern entrance were initiated at this time, when attention seems to have shifted towards the site's solsticial alignment. Meanwhile, throughout this process, the ditch re-cutting continued. Eventually, a special place that had started life as a relatively small centre for regular local gatherings was starting to develop into something altogether more remarkable. If we are correct in our supposition that the ditch was indeed ultimately derived from that of a causewayed enclosure, then the centuries between 3300 and 3000 BC were the time when Stonehenge began to acquire its new and unique identity.

We have already discussed radiocarbon dates from the Stonehenge ditch that suggest it was probably initially dug well before 2900 BC. Another strand of evidence that hints at an earlier date is provided by radiocarbon results from three cremations from the huge cemetery enclosed by the ditch. In round terms, these can be dated to the years between 3300 and 2900 BC.[192]

One reason for the seeming confusion has been the widespread adoption of a sophisticated statistical technique, known as Bayesian modelling, which allows several radiocarbon measurements to be taken together in order to provide a more precise and reliable series of dates for various ancient monuments.[193] It has been adopted in archaeology over the past two decades with great success. The technique, however, depends on being able to find layers in the ground that can be identified with closely definable stages in a particular site or monument's construction, followed by its use and, finally, its demise.[194] Normally that is quite straightforward. But not always. When Bayesian modelling began for Stonehenge, it was assumed that the digging of the ditch took place in a single event, as does indeed seem to have been the case with other henges. But what if Stonehenge was different?

We know that Stonehenge was one of the earliest of the so-called 'formative' henges, and the ditch does show clear links with causewayed enclosures, which we know in many cases were never 'constructed' in a single event at all, but came into existence more gradually as different families or communal groups set to work digging their individual ditch segments. It is generally assumed that the initial digging of the Stonehenge ditch took place as part of a single event or ceremony. But there is no archaeological evidence to support this. Indeed, the near-constant re-cutting that is such a feature of the subsequent history of the various ditch segments strongly recalls what happened a few centuries earlier at causewayed enclosures. It could be suggested that although slightly later, the different segments of the ditch would have been excavated and subsequently re-cut to celebrate significant events in the social history of individual kin, or family, groups (for example, an elder dies and is commemorated). There is no reason to suppose that such small-scale gatherings would yet have been closely co-ordinated between different communities. The same probably goes, too, for the huge number of cremations that are distributed across the ground enclosed by the ditch, some of which we have seen to be early. Everything about this initial phase at Stonehenge suggests a degree of local autonomy without strong central control.

If the initial digging and subsequent re-cutting of the Stonehenge ditch did not happen as a single one-off 'launching' event, then the Bayesian modelling of the radiocarbon results is going to reject those dates that are perceived to fall outside that theoretical, and possibly non-existent, 'event'. And that is where I believe a mistake has been made. In its initial, formative phases, Stonehenge still belonged to an earlier[*] tradition of less co-ordinated communal action, where well-planned, large-scale 'events' as such were rare. This phase sees the digging and frequent re-cutting of the ditch segments and the use of the site as a cremation cemetery. Some of the timber structures may date to this formative phase, too.

It is harder to pin down precisely when the change from less to more co-ordination happened. The regular spacing of the Aubrey Holes suggests greater control, but the fact that they cross the main entranceway also implies that the solsticial alignment had yet to be stressed or re-emphasized. Further,

---

[*]   Prehistorians would refer to this as a Middle Neolithic tradition. The main construction and use of Stonehenge is firmly Late Neolithic, Copper Age and Early Bronze Age.

the quarrying and collection of the bluestones is another early expression of a more co-ordinated use of labour and the landscape. But again, the change from local to a more centralized form of control does not need to have been sudden. Indeed, there may have been more than one 'event' to mark the transition. New data is urgently needed to clarify this – perhaps by re-examining the disturbed lengths of ditch excavated by Hawley.

In this book I have separated the earliest, less formal and more spontaneous developments at Stonehenge (the digging of the ditch segments and the cremations, plus some of the timber structures) from what I perceive to be the more formal developments of Stage 1, which included the final re-cutting of the ditch, the Aubrey Holes and work associated with the solstice-aligned main entranceway. I have called these initial episodes the Formative Phase and I have suggested that they probably started around 3300 BC with the first digging of the enclosing ditch. The first, formal stage (Stage 1) is marked by the final re-cutting of the ditch and the elaboration of the solstice-aligned northeastern entranceway. Current radiocarbon dates suggest that these events probably began shortly before 2900 BC.

ACKNOWLEDGEMENTS

This book would not have been possible without the help and advice of Professor Mike Parker Pearson. I am also deeply indebted to Dr Josh Pollard who kindly read and commented on a draft, although of course I alone am responsible for any errors or omissions. Richard Milbank, Publishing Director, Non-Fiction, at Head of Zeus, has offered me most sympathetic guidance whenever it was needed. I would also like to thank Georgina Blackwell and Clemence Jacquinet at Head of Zeus; copyeditor Clare Cock-Starkey; designer Isambard Thomas and indexer Nick Nicholas. Finally, best thanks are due to my agent, Bill Hamilton of A.M. Heath and Co. My wife Maisie deserves special gratitude for her forbearance, when her own work on the timbers at Star Carr was disrupted, because her photographic assistant's brain was forever lodged on Salisbury Plain.

Stone 'Enge on Salisbury Plain, 1784 by Thomas Rowlandson (1756–1827).

NOTES

PROLOGUE:
WHY STONEHENGE MATTERS

1 Bowden, M., Soutar, S., Field, D. and Barber, M. (2015), *The Stonehenge Landscape: Analysing the Stonehenge World Heritage Site* (Historic England, Swindon).

2 The two contenders would be the complex of sites on Mainland Orkney and around Avebury, in Wiltshire.

INTRODUCTION: RELIGION, LANDSCAPE AND CHANGE

3 Pollard, J and Ruggles, C. (2001), 'Shifting Perceptions: Spatial Order, Cosmology, and Patterns of Deposition at Stonehenge', *Cambridge Archaeological Journal*, Vol 11:1, pp. 69–90. Pollard, J. (2009), 'The Materialization of Religious Structures in the Time of Stonehenge', *Material Religion*, vol. 5, pp. 332–353.

4 Whittle, A., Healy, F. and Bayliss, A. (2011), *Gathering Time: Dating the Early Neolithic Enclosures of Southern Britain and Ireland*, p. 839 (Oxbow Books, Oxford).

5 Smith, Isobel (1965), *Windmill Hill and Avebury: Excavations by Alexander Keiller 1925–1939* (Oxford University Press).

CHAPTER 1:
AFTER THE ICE

6 Milner, N., Taylor, B., Conneller, C., and Schadla-Hall, T. (2013), *Star Carr: Life in Britain After the Ice Age* (Council for British Archaeology, York).

7 For a graph of average temperature fluctuations over time see Scarre, C. (2005), *The Human Past: World Prehistory and the Development of Human Societies*, p.178, fig. 5.1 (Thames and Hudson, London).

8 The name was first used by Bryony Coles (1998), 'Doggerland: A Speculative Survey', *Proceedings of the Prehistoric Society*, 64, pp. 45–81.

9 Gaffney, V., Thomson, K., and Fitch, S. (2007), *Mapping Doggerland: The Mesolithic Landscapes of the Southern North Sea* (Archaeopress, Oxford).

10 The house and settlement are described in detail in Conneller, C., Milner, N., Taylor, B. and Taylor, M. (2012), 'Substantial Settlement in the European Early Mesolithic: New Research at Star Carr', *Antiquity*, Vol. 86, pp. 1004–1020.

11 For plans and sections of both the 1966 and 1988 car park extension excavations see Cleal, M. J., Walker, K. E., and Montague, R. (1995), *Stonehenge in its Landscape: Twentieth-Century Excavations*, pp. 42–7, Archaeological Report 10 (English Heritage, London).

12 Woodman, P. C. (1985), *Excavations at Mount Sandel, 1973–1977*, Archaeological Research Monographs No. 2 (Belfast).

13 Cleal et al. (1995) op. cit., Chapter 2.

14 The standard non-academic account is by the Stonehenge Riverside Project's Director, Professor Mike Parker Pearson (2012), *Stonehenge: Exploring the Greatest Stone Age Mystery* (Simon and Schuster, London). A shorter, more recent and superbly illustrated account is also available: Mike Parker Pearson (2015), *Stonehenge: Making Sense of a Prehistoric Mystery*. Archaeology for All series (Council for British Archaeology, York).

15 Josh Pollard, pers. comm.

16 'Early Mesolithic Cemetery', PAST (Newsletter of the Prehistoric Society), no. 69, p. 6 (November, 2011).

17 Parker Pearson op. cit. (2012), p. 236.

18 Jacques, D., and Phillips, T. (2014), 'Mesolithic settlement near Stonehenge: excavations at Blick Mead, Vespasian's Camp, Amesbury', *Wiltshire Archaeological and Natural History Magazine*, vol. 107, pp. 7–27. See also 'Blick Mead's Mesolithic home comforts', *Current Archaeology*, issue 310 (2016), p. 11.

19 Ibid., p. 23.

20 Ibid., p. 8.

CHAPTER 2:
THE STONEHENGE ´RITUAL LANDSCAPE´

21 Pryor, F. M. M. (2001) *Seahenge: A Quest for Life and Death in Bronze Age Britain* (HarperCollins, London). The

authoritative site report: Brennand, M., and Taylor, M. (2003), 'The Survey and Excavation of a Bronze Age Timber Circle at Holme-next-the-Sea, Norfolk, 1998–9', *Proceedings of the Prehistoric Society*, vol. 69, pp. 1–84.

22 Pryor op. cit. (2001), fig. 24, p. 241.

23 Robertson, D. (in press), 'A Second Timber Circle, Trackways and Coppicing at Holme-next-the-Sea Beach, Norfolk: Use of Salt- and Freshwater Marshes in the Bronze Age', *Proceedings of the Prehistoric Society*.

24 Lock, G. and Stancic, Z. (eds.) (1995), *Archaeology and GIS: A European Perspective* (Routledge, London).

25 Pryor, F. M. M. (2003), *Britain BC: Life in Britain and Ireland Before the Romans*, pp. 235–69 (HarperCollins, London).

26 Bradley, R. J. (1992), 'The gravels and British prehistory from the Neolithic to the Early Iron Age' in Fulford, M. and Nichols, E. (eds.), *Developing Landscapes of Lowland Britain. The Archaeology of the British Gravels: A Review*, pp. 15–22 (Society of Antiquaries of London, London). The paper that made the first impact: Royal Commission on Historic Monuments (1960), *A Matter of Time* (HMSO, London).

27 Bradley, R. J. (2000), *An Archaeology of Natural Places* (Routledge, London).

28 Pryor, F. M. M., and French, C. A. I. (1985), *Archaeology and Environment in the Lower Welland Valley*, Vol 1, East Anglian Archaeology Report No. 27 (Cambridge).

29   Richards, J. C. (1990), *The Stonehenge Environs Project*, English Heritage Archaeological Report No. 16 (Historic Buildings and Monuments Commission for England, London). For a more popular account see Richards, J. C. (1991), *English Heritage Book of Stonehenge*, (Batsford, London).

30   Richards, op. cit. (1990) pp. 40–61; fig. 97.

31   The Stonehenge Cursus is marked by two large pits at either end. These might well prove to be early. Josh Pollard, pers. comm.

32   Cleal et al. (1995) op. cit, fig. 33, pp. 57–8.

33   Pryor, F. M. M. (1998), *Etton: Excavations at a Neolithic causewayed enclosure near Maxey, Cambridgeshire, 1982–7*, English Heritage Archaeological Report No. 18 (London).

34   Whittle, A., Healy, F., and Bayliss, A. (2011), *Gathering Time: Dating the Early Neolithic Enclosures of Southern Britain and Ireland*, pp. 324–5 (Oxbow Books, Oxford).

35   Smith, I. F. (1965), *Windmill Hill and Avebury: Excavations by Alexander Keiller, 1925–1939* (Oxford University Press).

36   Thomas, N. de L. W. (1964), 'The Neolithic causewayed camp at Robin Hood's Ball, Shrewton.' *Wiltshire Archaeological and Natural History Magazine*, vol. 59, pp. 1–27.

37   Whittle et al. (2011) op. cit., pp. 200–3.

38   Parker Pearson, M. (2012) op. cit., pp. 138–41.

39   Pollard, J. and Reynolds, A. J. (2002), *Avebury: The biography of a landscape*, pp. 81–3, fig. 27 (Tempus, Stroud).

40   The Stonehenge Palisade, constructed from 1800 BC, forms a huge enclosure that includes both the Normanton Down barrows and Stonehenge itself, thereby emphasizing their inter-connectedness. Josh Pollard, pers. comm.

CHAPTER 3:
BEFORE THE GREAT STONES,
PART I: THE FORMATIVE STAGE

41   Oppenheimer, S. (2006), *The Origins of the British*, pp. 197–280 (Constable, London); Pryor, F. M. M. (2003) op. cit., Chapter 5 (with refs).

42   For example, Cleal et al. op. cit. (1995), figs. 40 and 42.

43   Mike Parker Pearson pers. comm. This is a revised date and replaces that given in Parker Pearson op. cit. (2012), pp. 191–2.

44   Josh Pollard, pers. comm.

45   Cleal et al. op. cit. (1995), figs. 67 and 68.

46   Ibid., p. 147 (C13, WA 2380).

47   Ibid., pp. 150–2.

48   Pryor op. cit. (1998), pp. 98–9; fig. 102, F360, F645.

49   Ibid., pp. 366–8.

50   Parker Pearson op. cit. (2012), plan p. 44.

51   A note on the dating of the Stages of Stonehenge as suggested here. The dates are based on Parker Pearson op. cit. (2015), but with small changes. The Formative Stage is new. I have taken the digging of the Aubrey Holes and the insertion of Bluestones into them, rather than the harder-to-pin-down re-cutting of the ditch, as the start date for Stonehenge Stage 1, which moves back a century from 2900 BC. The dating of the digging of the Aubrey Holes is based on a radiocarbon date for AH32 of 3080–2890 BC (Parker Pearson, pers. comm.).

CHAPTER 4:
BEFORE THE GREAT STONES, PART
II: STAGE 1

52   The site is now in the care of the National Trust.

53   Parker Pearson op. cit. (2012), pp. 292–302.

54   Ibid., p. 295.

55   Ibid., pp. 150–5.

56   Cummins, W. A. (1974), 'The Neolithic Stone Axe Trade in Britain', *Antiquity*, Vol. 48, pp. 201–5.

57   Sahlins, M., (1974), *Stone Age Economics* (Tavistock Publications, London).

58   Bradley, R. J. (2000), *An Archaeology of Natural Places* (Routledge, London).

59   Atkinson, R. J. C. (1979), *Stonehenge* (Penguin, Harmondsworth).

60   Richards, J. C. (1991), *English Heritage Book of Stonehenge*, p. 55 (Batsford/English Heritage, London).

61   Parker Pearson, M., Pollard, J., Richards, C., Schlee, D. and Welham, K. (2015), 'In search of the Stonehenge quarries', *British Archaeology*, 146 (Jan/Feb), pp. 16–23.

62   In Spanish: *Feria de abril de Sevilla*.

63   Brennand and Taylor op. cit. (2003).

64   From, John Aubrey's *Monumenta Britannica*; quoted in Cleal et al., op cit. (1995), p. 94. There is some doubt whether the Aubrey Holes are indeed the actual cavities noted by John Aubrey – see Pitts, M. W. (1981), 'Stones, pits and Stonehenge', *Nature*, vol. 290, p. 47. Josh Pollard (pers. comm.) has suggested that as 1666 was a hot, dry year (which helps explain the rapid spread of the Great Fire of London), the Aubrey Holes could have been revealed as dry patches, known to archaeologists as 'parch marks'.

65   Table 10 in Cleal et al., op. cit. (1995) shows that twenty-four of the thirty-two Aubrey Holes excavated by Hawley contained undoubted cremations.

66   The date was taken from a cremation in Aubrey Hole 32. Parker Pearson pers. comm, November, 2015.

67   Parker Pearson op. cit. (2015), p. 79.

68   Cleal et al., op. cit. (1995) fig. 93. It could have been broken in antiquity (ibid., p. 194).

69   And it is superbly described in Parker Pearson op. cit. (2012), chapter 15.

70   Ibid., p. 228.

CHAPTER 5:
THE GREAT STONES ARRIVE:
STAGE 2

71   Richards, op cit. (1990) and Cleal et al. op. cit. (1995).

72   The theory was published in two papers: Parker Pearson, M. and Ramilisonina (1998a), 'Stonehenge for the ancestors: the stones pass on the message', *Antiquity*, vol. 72, 308–26; Parker Pearson, M. and Ramilisonina (1998b), 'Stonehenge for the ancestors: part 2', *Antiquity*, vol. 72, 855–6.

73   Cunnington, M. E. (1929), *Woodhenge* (Simpson, Devizes).

74   Wainwright, G. J and Longworth, I. H. (1971), *Durrington Walls: Excavations 1966–1968* (Society of Antiquaries, London).

75   Parker Pearson op. cit. (2012) p. 157.

76   Abbott, M. and Anderson-Whymark, H., (2012) *Stonehenge Laser Scan: Archaeological Analysis Report*, Research Report No. 32 (Historic England, London).

77   Ibid., pp. 18–21.

78   Maisie Taylor pers. comm. Brennand and Taylor, op. cit. (2003), table 2; p. 65.

79   Abbott. and Anderson-Whymark op. cit. (2012), pp. 21–4.

80   A number of uprights in both the Sarsen Circle and Trilithon Horseshoe were re-erected or straightened in the twentieth Century. Cleal et al. (1995), Chapter 2.

81   Abbott and Anderson-Whymark op. cit. (2012), p. 50. The above-ground symmetry, however, was achieved at the

expense of the foundations, which were often too shallow – which would explain why so many of the upright stones have subsequently leant-over or toppled; see Parker Pearson, op. cit. (2015), p.111.

82   Abbott and Anderson-Whymark op. cit. (2012), p. 50–1.

83   Chippindale, C. (1983), *Stonehenge Complete*, p. 79 (Thames and Hudson, London).

84   Ibid., Chapter 14 – 'The Moon Behind the Megaliths'. A wonderful title!

85   Hawkins, G. S. with White, J. B. (1965), *Stonehenge Decoded* (Delta Books, New York).

86   Chippindale op. cit. (1983), p. 221.

87   Parker Pearson op. cit. (2012) plan p. 47. For even more possibilities see Chippindale op. cit. (1983), pp. 221–3.

88   Parker Pearson op. cit. (2015), pp. 26–7.

89   Atkinson op. cit. (1978), pp. 58–61; fig. 3 (centre).

90   Which are also being slowly discovered. Pryor, F. M. M. (2010), *The Making of the British Landscape*, pp. 521–2 (Penguin, London).

91   Parker Pearson op. cit. (2012), Chapters 3 and 4.

92   Ibid., Chapter 5.

93   I describe the village in Pryor, F. M. (2014), *HOME: A Time Traveller's Tales from British Prehistory*, pp. 107–13, 115–7

94   This account of the Durrington Walls village and henge draws extensively on Parker Pearson op. cit. (2015) and (2012), chapters 5–7.

95   Pryor, F. M. M. (1984), *Excavation at Fengate, Peterborough, England: The Fourth Report*, Royal Ontario Museum Monograph 7/Northants. Archaeological Society Monograph 2, fig 16 (Northampton and Toronto).

96   Parker Pearson op. cit. (2015), p. 51.

97   Craig, O. E., Shillito, L-M., Albarella, U., Viner-Daniels, S., Chan, B., Cleal, R.,

Ixer, R., Jay, M., Marshall, P., Simmons, E., Wright, E. and Parker Pearson, M. (2015), 'Feeding Stonehenge: cuisine and consumption at the Late Neolithic site of Durrington Walls', *Antiquity*, 89, pp. 1096–1109.

CHAPTER 6:
THE JOURNEY FROM LIFE TO DEATH:
STAGE 3

98   For images of the newly-discovered stone row go to: http://www.lbiarchpro-imagery.at/stonehenge2015 For Durrington Avenue see Parker Pearson op. cit. (2015), pp. 51–6.

99   Parker Pearson op. cit. (2012), p. 222.

100   Evans, J. G. (1984), 'Stonehenge – The Environment in the Late Neolithic and Early Bronze Age and a Beaker-Age Burial', *Wiltshire Archaeological and Natural History Magazine*, vol. 78, pp. 7–30.

101   Ibid., figs. 13 and 14.

102   Pryor, F. M. M. (1980), *Excavation at Fengate, Peterborough, England: The Third Report*, pls. 4 and 12 (Royal Ontario Museum/Northants Archaeology, Toronto and Northampton).

103   Fitzpatrick, A. P. (2002), "The Amesbury Archer': a well-furnished Early Bronze Age burial in southern England', *Antiquity*, Vol. 76, No. 293, pp. 629–30.

104   Cleal, R. M. J. (2011), 'Pottery', in Fitzpatrick op. cit. (2011), pp. 140–54.

105   McKinley, J. I. (2011), 'Human Remains (graves 1236 and 1289)', in Fitzpatrick op. cit. (2011), pp. 77–87.

106   Chenery, C. A. and Evans, J. A. (2011), 'Isotope Analyses', in Fitzpatrick op. cit. (2011), p. 87.

107   Josh Pollard, pers. comm.

CHAPTER 7:
LATER DEVELOPMENTS:
STAGES 4 AND 5

108   Cleal et al. op. cit. (1995), pp. 307–11.

109   Parker Pearson op. cit. (2012), pp. 311–2; Cleal et al. op. cit. (1995), pp. 356–65.

110   Atkinson, op. cit. (1979), p. 84.

111   Parker Pearson op. cit. (2012), p. 347.

112   Needham, S., Lawson, A. J. and Woodward, A. (2010), "A noble group of barrows': Bush Barrow and the Normanton Down Early Bronze Age cemetery two centuries on'. *Antiquaries Journal*, vol. 90, pp. 1–39.

113   Tourist damage can often be very substantial, which is why modern visitors have to be kept outside the Stones. For an accurate record of damage caused by visitors, see Abbott and Anderson-Whymark op. cit. (2012), pp. 42–7.

114   Cleal et al. op. cit. (1995), p. 30. Atkinson op cit. (1979), p. 44.

115   Abbott and Anderson-Whymark op. cit. (2012), p. 26.

116   See, for example, Pearce, S. M. (1983), *The Bronze Age Metalwork of South Western England*, 2 vols., British Archaeological Reports, British Series Vol 120; Moore, C. N and Rowlands, M. (1972), *Bronze Age Metalwork in Salisbury Museum*, Plate VI (Salisbury Museum); Harbison, P. (1969), *The Axes of the Early Bronze Age in Ireland* (Beck, Munich)

117   Abbott and Anderson-Whymark op. cit. (2012), p. 37.

118   Ibid.

119   Brennand and Taylor, op. cit. (2003), pp. 82–4.

CHAPTER 8:
AFTER THE STONES

120   Pryor, F. M. M., op. cit. (2014), p. 169.

121   Pryor, F. M. M. (2006), *Farmers in Prehistoric Britain*, 2nd Ed. (Tempus, Stroud); Yates, D. T. (2001), 'Bronze Age Agricultural Intensification in the Thames Valley and Estuary', in Brück, J. (ed.), *Bronze Age Landscapes: Tradition and Transformation*, pp. 65–82 (Oxbow Books, Oxford); Yates, D. T. (2007), *Land, Power and Prestige: Bronze Age Field Systems in Southern England* (Oxbow Books, Oxford).

122   Thames (Latin *Tamesis*): 'An ancient Celtic river name, possibly meaning 'dark one'.' Other rivers that share this root are the Thame (three examples), Team (Durham), Thame (Bucks.) and Tamar (Devon–Cornwall). Mills, A. D. (1991), *A Dictionary of English Place Names*, p. 324 (Oxford University Press).

123   The developed phase consisted of the later Bronze and Iron Ages.

124   Cunliffe, B. W. (2005), *Iron Age Communities in Britain*, 4th Ed., pp. 355–7 (Oxford University Press); Hunter-Mann, K. (1999), 'Excavations at Vespasian's Camp Iron Age hillfort, 1987', *Wiltshire Archaeological and Natural History Magazine*, vol. 92, pp. 39–52.

125   They were mapped in an innovative landscape study by Julian Richards. See Richards, op. cit. (1990), fig. 160.

126   Ibid., p. 279.

127   E.g. Cleal et al. op. cit. (1995), p. 334.

128   Ibid., p. 434.

129   For the Aubrey Holes see ibid., pp. 99–101; for Romano-British pottery in general see ibid., p. 435.

130   Ibid., p. 260.

131   Mills, op. cit. (1991), p. 311.

132   E.g. Parker Pearson op. cit. (2015), p. 125.

133   Cleal et al. op. cit. (1995), p. 205.

134   Parker Pearson op. cit. (2015), p. 33.

135   Cleal at al. op. cit. (1995), p. 339.

136   Ibid., Chapter 8.

137   Ibid., fig. 188.

138 Abbott and Anderson-Whymark op. cit. (2012), pp. 38–47.

139 Ibid., p. 39.

140 Pitts, M. W. (2001), *Hengeworld*, p. 82 (Arrow Books, London).

141 Abbott and Anderson-Whymark op. cit. (2012), pp. 45–7.

142 Ibid., p. 44.

143 Quoted from Wheeler, R. E. M. (1956), *Archaeology from the Earth*, p. 15 (Penguin, Harmondsworth).

144 The following account of early research into Stonehenge draws heavily on Cleal et al. op. cit. (1995), Chapter 2.

145 Gowland, W. (1902), 'Recent Excavations at Stonehenge', *Archaeologia*, vol. 58, pp. 37–105.

146 Cleal et al. op. cit. (1995), p. 13.

147 If the view of Hawley's project given here is thought severe, Chippindale op. cit. (1983) names his chapter (12) on Hawley 'The Destruction of Half Stonehenge'.

148 Cleal et al. op. cit. (1995), pp. 12–15.

149 Ibid., p. 15.

150 Ibid., p. 19.

151 Atkinson, R. J. C., Piggott, S. and Stone, J. F. S. (1952), 'The excavation of two additional holes at Stonehenge, and new evidence for the date of the monument', *Antiquaries Journal*, vol. 32, pp. 14–20.

152 Atkinson op. cit (-).

153 Cleal et al. op. cit. (1995).

154 Ibid., appendix 9.

155 Darvill, T. (2005), *Stonehenge World Heritage Site: An Archaeological Research Framework* (English Heritage and Bournemouth University, London and Bournemouth).

CHAPTER 9:
STONEHENGE TODAY

156 The word is a Greek term, *eikon*, meaning 'image'.

157 The cover blurb of Chippindale op. cit. (1983) is unusually accurate: 'Everything important, interesting or odd that has been written or painted, discovered or imagined, about the most extraordinary ancient building in the world.'

158 Cleal et al. op. cit. (1995).

159 An excellent illustrated version was published in 1982. See Morris, C. (ed.) (1982), *The Illustrated Journeys of Celia Fiennes, c.1682–c.1712* (Webb and Bower, Exeter).

160 We know she had read William Camden's *Britannia* (1586). This county-by-county survey of its landscape and monuments is arguably the first serious archaeological study of Britain. It was extensively revised and enlarged throughout the seventeenth century and she would have read a later version, in English (the first edition was in Latin). Ibid., p. 27.

161 Ibid., pp. 42–3

162 Alfred Watkins (1925), *The Old Straight Track*, new introduction by Robert Macfarlane (2014), p. xxiv (Head of Zeus, London).

163 Ibid., figs. 104 and 105.

164 For the complex history of the 1655 publication see Chippindale op. cit. (1983), p. 278, n.17.

165 Ibid., p. 105.

166 Ibid.

167 But it has been a controversial process. For the latest problems see Hill, R. (2015), 'The Battle of Stonehenge', *The Oldie*, issue 324, pp. 26–8.

APPENDIX II:
THE DITCH AND THE GRADUAL
ESTABLISHMENT OF STONEHENGE

168 Cleal et al. op. cit. (1995), pp. 65–94.

169 Smith op. cit. (1965), p. xx.

170 They were labelled Phases 1A (the earliest), 1B, 1C and 2 (the latest). Pryor op. cit. (1998), pp. 18–19; Chapter 12; Chapter 16.

171 Cleal et al. op. cit. (2011), fig. 6.32. With hindsight I now realize that the three phases might be somewhat over-defined as a result of the Bayesian statistics employed. In the field it was not always possible to be completely certain about a given layer's phasing.

172 For example, Pryor op. cit. (1998), figs. 39, 43–4.

173 For example, Cleal et al. op. cit. (2011), figs 44–7.

174 Etton ditch segment 9, layer 3. See Pryor op. cit. (1998), figs 39–41.

175 This can be clearly seen in segment 9, layer 2, where the edge of the relatively narrow recut helps confine the placed deposits (ibid., figs. 37–8).

176 Inverted round-bottom bowls placed at causeways were also thought to represent human heads at the Danish causewayed enclosure at Sarup. Andersen, N. H. (1997), *Sarup vol. 1: The Sarup Enclosures*, fig. 262, p.225 (Aarhus University Press).

177 For the sea urchin see ibid., figs. 33–5.

178 Ibid., pp. 47–8.

179 Ibid., p. 49.

180 Compare Pryor op. cit. (1998), fig. 206 with Cleal et al. op. cit. (1995), fig. 194.

181 It is mostly Beaker and Bronze Age. See Cleal et al. op. cit. (1995), figs. 195–8.

182 For the animal bones see ibid., p. 71; for the antler, ibid., p. 87 (C26, Section 26.5).

183 Ibid., p.74 (segment 99).

184 Ibid., p. 83 (section C18.3: 1269).

185 See, for example, ibid., p. 83, p. 87, p. 91 (Newall's drawing).

186 The undulations are clearly visible in the plan, ibid., p.81 and the photograph (ibid., p. 93).

187 Bamford, H. M. (1985), *Briar Hill: Excavations 1974–1978* (Northampton Development Corporation, Northampton).

188 Ibid., pp. 7–9.

189 Whittle et al. op. cit. (2011), p. 694.

190 One rim sherd of undecorated Early Neolithic pottery was found in the ditch bank: Cleal et al. op. cit. (1995), p. 60.

191 At Etton, for example, the three known principal entranceways faced roughly north, east and west.

192 3340–2940, 3330–2920 and 3310–2910 BC. Information kindly provided by Mike Parker Pearson.

193 The technique is named after its inventor, the eighteenth-century statistician and cleric Thomas Bayes (1702–61).

194 I am grateful to Josh Pollard for reminding me of this.

INDEX

A

aerial surveys   33, 49, 103
altar rails   107
altars   22
Amesbury Archer   134–36
animals   18, 40, 55, 58, 83, 118
antlers   31, 143, 192, 193
archery   131, 133, 134
astronomical alignments   77, 113, 115, 174
Atkinson, Professor Richard   115, 143, 149
Aubrey Holes   73, 91–93, 166, 197
Aubrey, John   91
aurochs (wild cattle)   40, 42, 55, 192
Avebury   23, 49, 61
Avenue, the   37, 104, 142, 143, 166
Avon, River   32, 37, 87, 95, 103–4, 126–27
axes   85–86, 110, 130, 131
Ayers Rock   50

B

banks   62, 70–73, 77, 91, 114, 127
barrow mounds   57–58, 62, 65, 115, 142, 146–47
Bayesian modelling   196
Beckhampton Avenues   64
Bell Beakers   131, 133, 136, 137
Blick Mead   39–43
Bluestonehenge   95, 103, 115, 126–30, 161
bluestones
    placing   115, 142
    quarrying   82, 93, 108, 198
    symbolism   128–30
    transportation   87, 90
bones   32, 40, 61, 101, 121, 192
boundaries, rivers as   55, 156
Briar Hill, Northampton   193

Bristol Channel   87
Bronze Age (2200–800 BC)   62, 64, 134, 137, 142–51, 159, 161
burial mounds   23, 48, 54, 64
burials   39, 133–34, 136, 151
Bush Barrow   148

C

cairns   58, 156
carvings   149–51, 156
causewayed enclosures   12, 58, 77, 101, 188, 194–97
ceremonial routes   103, 126–27, 143
Chalcolithic period   18, 58, 104, 130
chalk   37, 118, 143, 193
circular ditches   61–62, 70–77
communities   58, 134, 158–59, 194
Coneybury Henge   55
conflict   134, 158
Constable, John   174–76, 176
copper   18, 131
corn-grinding stones (querns)   61
Craig Rhos-y-felin quarry   93
cremation cemeteries   72, 77, 93, 104
Cunningham, Maud   103
Cunningham, William   146
cursuses   62, 64

D

deer   55, 143
Deller, Jeremy   177
ditches   37–38, 61–62, 70–77, 115, 188–97, 198
Doggerland   30–31
dogs   18, 58

Domestic Revolution   156–60
Durrington Walls   103–4, 116–17, 126, 143, 179

E

eclipses   20, 113
entranceways   48, 94, 127, 195, 198
erosion   38, 116
Etton, Welland Valley   58, 64, 71, 85–86, 189–93
Europe   17, 131, 136–37

F

farming   48, 49, 54–55, 134, 142, 156, 158–59
feasting   40, 55, 61, 194
Fiennes, Celia   172–73
Flag Fen, Peterborough (Iron Age village)   177
flax (string)   58, 193
flint   18, 32, 39, 40, 55
Flixton, Yorkshire   31
flood-plains   32, 40, 159
Foamhenge (created for Channel 5's Stonehenge Live)   93, 128, 176
forensic examinations   136
Formative Stage   55, 70–77, 91, 94, 101, 198
foundations   160
furnaces   131

G

GIS (Geographic Information Systems)   49
Gowland, Professor William   165
grave goods   58, 131, 133, 134–36, 146–47
Great Stones   82
Great Trilithon   109, 110, 112, 160
Greater Cursus   62
greenstone axes   85, 86, 130
Greylake, Somerset   39
Grooved Ware   192
grooves, rippled   85, 109
gullies, natural   38, 43, 50

H

Hawkins, Gerald S.   113
Hawley, Lt.-Col. William   73, 91–93, 143, 165, 189, 195
Heel Stone   37, 74, 115, 162
henges   62–64, 77, 103–4, 116–18, 190
hillforts   158
Hoare, Sir Richard Colt   146
houses   31–32, 117–21
human skulls   58, 191
hunter-gatherers   18, 38, 40, 43

I

Ice Age   82, 87
Iron Age (800 BC–AD 43)   86, 137, 156, 158, 159
Iron Age village   118

J

Jacques, David   40, 42
jewellery   133, 134, 146–47
Jones, Inigo   174

L

Lake District   86, 130
Lake Flixton   32
landscape   39, 42, 94–95, 158, 173
Langdale quarries   86, 130
laser-scan surveys   109, 110, 112, 149, 161
Lesser Cursus   62
ley lines   173, 174
lichen growth   109
'liminal' places   86, 130
lintels   82, 94, 107, 112
Lockeridge Dene, Marlborough   83

M

maceheads   148
Madagascar   100
Marlborough Downs   82, 83
Maxey Cursus   64, 190
megaliths   82, 87
Mesolithic period   17, 18, 31, 34–35, 70
metal-working   131, 149
Middle Ages   23
Middle Neolithic   195
monoliths   37
monuments, 'invisible'   33

N

'Neolithic computer'   113
Neolithic period   18, 42, 55, 62, 70, 72
networks, local   158
New Order   156
Newall, Robert   165
Normanton Down   64–65, 146–47
North Barrow   114, 174
North Sea   30

O

oak trees   34, 48, 110
offerings   130, 143, 156, 191–93, 195
oilfields, Norwegian   30–31
Old Straight Track, The (Alfred Watkins)   173–74
outcrops   50, 87

P

paintings   174–76, 176
Palisade   39
Parker Pearson, Mike   42, 93, 100–1, 103, 116
Passageway   74, 76
photographic archives   71, 166
pigs   55, 121
pine trees   33, 34, 42, 74
pits   33, 34, 55
Pitts, Dr Mike   176
ploughing   37, 49, 143
post-holes   32, 34, 73–74, 126
post-Ice Age   18, 30–31
posts   33–35, 42, 74, 76, 103, 118, 126
pottery   55, 58, 61, 131, 159, 195
Preseli Mountains, Pembrokeshire   87, 130

Q

querns (corn-grinding stones)   61, 191

R

radar surveys   33
Ramilisonina (archaeologist)   100–1, 101, 116
religion   17, 19, 23, 50, 156
Richards, Julian   55
rites of passage
   ancestors   61, 146
   death   22–23, 57, 101
   importance   54
   marriages   137, 194
ritual landscapes   24, 48–50, 54–55, 103, 142, 158
rivers, as boundaries   55, 156
roads   33, 103, 177

Robin Hood's Ball   61
Roman architecture   174
Roman period   137, 159
ropes, honeysuckle   91
rubble mounds (cairns)   58, 156

S

Sacrilege (Jeremy Deller)   177
Salisbury Museum   167
Salisbury Plain   39, 49, 55, 82, 130
sandstone   82
Sarsen Circle   25, 94, 107–11, 142, 161, 179
sarsen hammer-stones   85
sarsen stones   82–85, 90, 109, 143, 173
Scheduled Ancient Monuments   103
sea levels   30, 31, 190
Seahenge, Norfolk   48, 110, 151
seismic surveys   31
semi-circular ditches   115
sheep   83
shrines   24, 48, 50, 71, 156
Silbury Hill   49
single-graves   133
site records   166
Slaughter Stone   93, 115
social status   133, 151, 194
soil examinations   38
solsticial alignments   48, 64, 112, 126, 156, 174
South Barrow   115, 174
spiritual worlds   20, 22, 50, 101
springs, natural   40, 50
Star Carr settlement   31, 32
Station Stones   115
stone-dressing   83, 85, 93, 109, 110, 112
stone-holes   74, 91, 94, 115, 126, 127
Stonehenge Decoded (Gerald S. Hawkins)   113
Stonehenge Environs Project   55
Stonehenge in its Landscape:
   Twentieth-century Excavations
   (English Heritage)   100, 161, 166
Stonehenge Riverside Project   35–39, 83, 87, 103, 116–18, 126
Stonehenge Stages   82–95, 100–21, 126–37, 142–48, 198
   See also Formative Stage
Stonehenge World Heritage Site   146
summer solstice   37, 64, 87, 94, 115, 174
symbolism

Ayers Rock (Uluru)   50
chalk balls   193
humans and   128–30, 191
stones   101, 116
timber   116, 126
water   50

T

Thames Valley   49
timber circles   48, 103, 126
Time Team (TV programme)   91
tombs   57, 86, 100–1, 101, 149
trade   86
transportation   90–91
tree-ring dating   48
trees   33, 34, 42, 74, 110
trench, car park   33–35, 42
Trilithon Horseshoe   25, 107, 110–11, 142, 149

V

Vespasian's Camp   39, 40, 158
viewsheds   49, 64
Visitor Centre   33, 177, 178

W

Wainwright, Geoffrey   103
water   40, 50, 136, 156
Watkins, Alfred   173–74
weaponry   58, 131, 133, 146–47
Welland, River   190
West Amesbury henge   127
West Kennet Long Barrow   57
Windmill Hill, Avebury   61, 189
winter solstice   37, 64, 110, 115, 126
Woodhenge   101, 103, 103–4, 130, 143

Y

Y and Z Holes   143

STONEHENGE

Pegasus Books Ltd
148 West 37th Street, 13th Fl
New York, NY 10018

Copyright © 2017 by Francis Pryor

First Pegasus Books hardcover edition February 2018

Designed and typeset by
Isambard Thomas, London

All rights reserved. No part of this book may be
reproduced in whole or in part without written
permission from the publisher, except by reviewers
who may quote brief excerpts in connection with a
review in a newspaper, magazine, or electronic
publication; nor may any part of this book be
reproduced, stored in a retrieval system, or transmitted
in any form or by any means electronic, mechanical,
photocopying, recording, or other, without written
permission from the publisher.

ISBN: 978-1-68177-640-8

10 9 8 7 6 5 4 3 2 1

Printed in the United States of America
Distributed by W. W. Norton & Company, Inc.

ILLUSTRATION CAPTIONS

pp.2–3
Stonehenge c.1827 by J. M. W. Turner (1775–1851).

p.4
A sixteenth century drawing of Stonehenge in
Corte Beschryvinghe van Engheland, Schotland, ende Irland
(Description of England, Scotland and Ireland).

pp.8–9
A photograph of visitors taking a rest at
Stonehenge in 1867.

p.183
An engraving of the prospect of Stonehenge from the
East and from the South, c.1684–85.

IMAGE CREDITS

pp.2–3 Salisbury Museum/Bridgeman Images;
p.4 British Library Board/Topfoto; pp.8–9 British Library
Board/Topfoto; pp.14–15 Shutterstock/Victor Kiev;
p.21 Private Collection/Bridgeman Images;
pp.26–7 © aerial-cam 2007; p.36 © aerial-cam 2008;
p.41 Wikimedia Commons; pp.44–5 Wikimedia
Commons; p.51 © Francis Pryor; p.52–3 Jeff Edwards; p.56
Corbis; p.59 © Francis Pryor; p.60 Salisbury,
Wiltshire/Bridgeman Images; p.63 © Liquid
Light/Alamy Stock Photo; pp.66–7 © Chris Beetles Ltd,
London/Bridgeman Images; p.72 Jeff Edwards;
p.75 British Library Board/Topfoto; pp.78–9 Private
Collection/Bridgeman Images; p.84 © Francis
Pryor; pp.88–9 © aerial-cam; pp.96–7 Private
Collection/The Stapleton Collection/Bridgeman
Images; p.102 Jeff Edwards; p.105 Jeff Edwards;
p.106 © The National Trust Photolibrary/Alamy Stock
Photo; p.108 Jeff Edwards; p.111 © Francis Pryor;
p.114 © aerial-cam; p.117 Jeff Edwards; p.119 © Francis
Pryor; p.120 © Francis Pryor; pp.122–3 Private Collection/©
Look and Learn/Bernard Platman Antiquarian
Collection/Bridgeman Images; p.129 © aerial-cam;
p.132 Jeff Edwards; p.135 © Wessex Archaeology;
pp.138–9 Ann Ronan Picture Library/Heritage
Images/Topfoto; pp.144–5 Jeff Edwards; p.147 © Francis
Pryor; p.150 Jeff Edwards; pp.152–3 Travel21
Impact/Heritage Images/Topfoto; p.157 © Wessex
Archaeology; p.163 Wiltshire Archaeological and Natural
History Society; p.166 Topfoto; pp.168–9 Wikimedia
Commons; p.175 © Francis Pryor; p.178 © Francis
Pryor; p.179 Victor Maschek/Shutterstock; pp.180–1
Wikimedia Commons; p.183 Society of Antiquaries of
London, UK/Bridgeman Images; p.187 Hulton
Archive/Getty Images; pp.200–1 Salisbury
Museum/Bridgeman Images.